"Seldom are persons allowed to peak behind the curtain of strong visionary leaders. Edgar Vann pulls it back for all to see how difficult it is to do the exceptional and the hidden cost paid by dreamers. Read it and take note! Honor the vision; preserve the visionary"

Bishop Walter S. Thomas, Sr.

"Bishop Vann has dedicated his life to the service of others. He has encouraged, inspired and tirelessly supported so many with his strong faith and personal message of hope. I have had the great pleasure of working together with Bishop Vann on numerous community projects and charitable causes. He is truly a man of outstanding character, and he is unselfish in his desire to uplift others and to make a lasting difference in everything he does."

Matt Simoncini, President and CEO of Lear Corporation

BISHOP EDGAR LEO VANN is one of the stalwart Fathers of the Christian Church for this Twenty-first Century. His outstanding leadership in Detroit has been a shining example of four decades of committed ministry to Christ and His people. BUT BISHOP VANN paid an awful price for the successes he acquired, and it took a heart attack, and a collapse in his work-station for him to call himself "an Overachiever." The Bishop labored as though he had been called to "success." We often wondered how he managed to be a best-friend to his bride (Sheila) and a super father to his son and daughter, while building a mega-ministry in a poverty-stricken community, and preach a sound, relevant, Spirit-filled message every week to a hurting people. Then, it happened! The lights suddenly went out and Edgar Vann laid helpless on a bed, forced to enter God's academy for "Overachievers." The lesson was; "God has not called you to success; but to faithfulness."

The second lesson was taught by Christ, Himself; "Come ye apart from yourselves and rest awhile." What a class that must have been! For if we don't "Come apart" we will soon "come apart!

I believe that Bishop Vann has caught ahold of several keys for our lives and ministries in this book; "I Did It to Myself!" The book must be a good read but certainly a helpful guidepost for those of us who serve Christ's causes.

J. DELANO ELLIS II

METROPOLITAN-ARCHBISHOP

JOINT COLLEGE OF AFRICAN-AMERICAN PENTECOSTAL BISHOPS

"Bishop Edgard Vann, one of our region's strongest spiritual voices, is also a powerful community leader and advocate who has improved the economic and physical health of Detroit and Michigan residents through decades of transformational community service. His new book, I did it to Myself; True Confessions of an Overachiever, gives us a front row look at a spiritual, yet human experience that changed his life and positively impacted thousands of others through his activism. It's a must read."

Daniel J. Loepp, President and CEO, Blue Cross Blue Shield of Michigan

A "sudden cardiac death" was the wake-up call for my friend, Bishop Vann, to take a close look at his life and reflect on the changes he had to make – and share that wisdom in this fine book. I Did It to Myself is like a "saving grace" for all those who feel out of balance and overwhelmed with trying to be superman or superwoman at work. Bishop Vann confesses that he was a workaholic, but no more. He is living his life on purpose and on point. In this book, he gives suggestions on how to weave rest, relaxation and reflection into our lives everyday without feeling guilty or falling behind in the really important work.

Dr. Geneva J. Williams, Author

Justice on the Jersey Shore

www.drgenevaspeaks.com

"This book is filled with important lessons and thoughtful insights for all of us who confess to being over-achievers. Bishop Vann was "made to lie down" in order to give him the opportunity to pause and discover what true work-life balance means. His book is an inspiring gift to all of us."

- U.S Senator Debbie Stabenow

EDGAR L. VANN

I DID IT TO MYSELF

TRUE CONFESSIONS OF AN
OVERACHIEVER

WESTBOW
PRESS®
A DIVISION OF THOMAS NELSON
& ZONDERVAN

WestBow Press books may be ordered through booksellers or by contacting:

WestBow Press
A Division of Thomas Nelson & Zondervan
1663 Liberty Drive
Bloomington, IN 47403
www.westbowpress.com
1 (866) 928-1240

ISBN: 978-1-9736-2644-2 (sc)
ISBN: 978-1-9736-2645-9 (hc)
ISBN: 978-1-9736-2643-5 (e)

Library of Congress Control Number: 2018904654

Print information available on the last page.

WestBow Press rev. date: 6/08/2018

CONTENTS

ACKNOWLEDGEMENTS

The very breath I breathe has a source. There can be no design, without a designer. There can be no structure without an architect. There can be no creation without a Creator. Preeminently, above all, I give glory and honor to God for all of His benefits toward me. A miracle was performed just for me and God is the source. Concurrently, it is His abiding grace and undeserved favor that makes this literary treatise possible. Writing this book challenged me to an unprecedented level of transparency. My back-to-life experience placed a demand on my normal proclivity of handling private matters in a guarded way. And so, in this book, I unearth areas of my life never publicly exposed. This book for me is simultaneously both catharsis and therapy.

My sincerest aspiration is that as my journey back-to-life brought healing to my body and soul, it does the very same for those who read it. May you be challenged to the very core of your being toward change and metamorphosis. May you conquer the burden of busyness and intently seek that which is essential.

I owe so many people a profound debt of gratitude for this book's completion.

My wife, Sheila is the love that permeates my life and completes me. In 40 years of marriage she has assumed multiple roles. My spiritual rock, the consummate mother and caregiver, my priceless friend, and the ultimate partner in love and ministry. Thank you.

Edgar III and Ericka Monique, my accomplished adult children. You brighten my life exponentially.

Rhonda Graves, my executive assistant for her professionalism and efficiency. Thank you for adding a special gift to my life.

Second Ebenezer Church, the people I've been called to lead for over 41 years. You've made me much of who I am.

Erica Terry, Felicia Foster-Gibson, Francesca McGhee, Ramona Berry and the Emergency Medical Response Team......Forever Grateful.

Anthony Neely, my "second pair of eyes;" a respected journalist whose editorial skills are impeccable.

Edward Boyd and Vikki Hardy-Brown, Connect the Dots Consulting; Pam Perry, Ministry Marketing Solutions; Angela Spenser-Ford, Shift 8 Degrees.

Great friends and mentors......Bishop T.D. Jakes, Dr. Frank E. Ray Sr., Dr. S.L. Jones, Bishop James R. Woodson, Bishop Liston Page, Jr. Bishop Walter Thomas, Bishop J. Delano Ellis II, Bishop Alfred A. Owens, Dr. Edward L. Branch, Dr. Christopher Brooks, Pastor Marcus Ways, Bishop J. Drew Sheard, Bishop Joseph W. Walker III, Pastors Reginald and Kelley Steele, Bishop James Williams, Kingdom Alliance Covenant Fellowship, and they rest eternally, Dr. Edgar L. Vann Sr. and Annie Louise Vann.

INTRODUCTION

I Did It to Myself is the product of a life-to-death and back-to-life experience that changed my perspective on the nature of work, career commitment, and ultimately the meaning of success. My steady and ongoing recovery from a medical emergency has made me more conscious of the need to delegate responsibility and to better value relationships. Most importantly, as pastor of a large church (Second Ebenezer Church in Detroit, Michigan) and a mentor and guide to other spiritual leaders, I've been forced to learn more about God's design for the proper balance of one's work life and personal life.

A lot of books, especially self-help and motivational books, are written to convince us to do more. They tell us: you've got to do this, you've got do that, you've got to multitask. People are told that to be successful, they've almost got to do everything all of the time—and squeeze in a bit of rest when they can. Isn't that the frenetic lifestyle into which our world is pushing us? We're pressured to take on more than we can, accelerate everything, and put undue time and extra due diligence into everything. We are encouraged to be all things to all people.

To be honest, that's how I've always looked at myself: as a multitalented multitasker, taking on many things at once. I had many gifts, abilities, talents, and skills, and I was able to do it all. Most of us have been raised to compartmentalize our lives. You get up. You go to work. You come home. You deal with what's happening at the house. You go to bed. You go back to work. It's a cycle that resembles a three-step process or a three-legged stool: basic, functional, but pretty limited. Life's beauty is really a matter of integrating all of its components into a fabric, a tapestry. The tapestry of life is what enhances its value and makes it attractive. But in many instances we've got it only compartmentalized; we don't have it integrated. And that's why it's not balanced.

Proper work-life integration is the answer. A complementary integration of our work lives and personal lives can help us open our eyes to the beauty we're missing. Whatever you're involved in, whatever you do, there's got to be a balance that you strike with it. I'm happy to say that in the aftermath of my life-threatening crisis, the second verse of the Bible's famous Twenty-Third Psalm has become reality to me: "He maketh me lie down in green pastures; He leadeth me beside the still waters." I have truly been made to lie down and compelled to slow down as part of my recovery.

I want to share with others the life-changing truths that I have learned and continue to learn. I'm most eager to reach those who are high achievers and who strive toward big goals, as I have for most of my life. Achieving work-life integration is my key message. That is the huge deliverable that should come out of *I Did It to Myself*. I want to teach successful people, overachievers, and people who take on great responsibility how important it is for them to truly balance their lives in the midst of all that they do. I think a lot of people from all walks of life need to hear such a message.

CHAPTER 1

AND THE CURTAIN FELL

My Sudden-Death Experience

It was December 31, 2015. Second Ebenezer Church held our annual New Year's Eve service, which is traditionally called Watch Night Service in African American churches across the country. Our service, like many others, is a time of preaching, prayer, and song that begins late in the evening and ends soon after midnight as a brand-new year is ushered in. Of course the church was packed—we had about three thousand people there. As bishop and pastor of the church, I led the service. By eleven thirty that evening, I was through preaching and came down from the stage to the main floor.

I had decided to do something different at midnight. I was going to distribute Holy Communion at midnight, which was not the normal routine for our church on New Year's Eve. Speaking from the main floor, I gave everyone instructions about how I wanted things done. I let everyone know that we would take an offering first. I told them to come to the front, give their offerings, and then receive their individually packaged communion sacraments and return to their seats. We would all partake of the wine (actually a swallow of grape juice in a miniature plastic cup) and the bread wafer at the same time, following my instructions from the pulpit. I stood there essentially winding down, not really exerting myself at all. All was well. My wife was standing with me. I had other assistants standing nearby, with officers holding offering buckets at each side of the main floor.

All of a sudden, it was just as if a black curtain was coming down in front of me. I knew I was going to pass out. It was like, *boom!* Darkness descended on me very fast. I reached for my wife and I grabbed her. And that was the last thing I remembered.

I was out and my heart stopped—no pulse—for about three minutes.

SUDDEN CARDIAC DEATH: A RARE FORM OF HEART FAILURE

My cardiologist told me later that I had experienced something called sudden cardiac death. Yes, death. That's what happened to me. I was told that only 5 to 10 percent of people who experience sudden cardiac death survive.

As explained by Dr. Nicea Goldberg, a prominent cardiologist who founded New York University's Joan Tisch Center for Women's Health and is a spokesperson for the American Heart Association, there is a big difference between two major types of heart failure: heart attack and sudden cardiac death.

> Heart failure occurs when the heart, which is essentially a pump, cannot effectively push blood out through the arteries and the circulatory system to the body's other organs and tissues. A heart attack is a circulatory problem, when circulation is blocked or cut off somehow, and when blood is no longer flowing to the heart muscle, which they call a myocardio infarction. Blockages in blood flow are caused by plaque building up in the arteries. Plaque forms when cholesterol combines with fat, calcium and other substances in the blood. That's the difference between heart failure and a heart attack.
>
> Sudden cardiac death is an electrical disturbance that causes the heart to suddenly stop beating. The heart's rhythm is erratic and irregular. Arrythmia causes it not to pump effectively, and as a result, you collapse. Sudden, unexpected loss of heart function results in

correspondent, sudden unexpected loss in breathing and consciousness. Survival rates for this (sudden cardiac death) are between 5 and 8 percent. CPR (cardio-pulmonary resuscitation) or chest compressions can save the life of one who suffers sudden cardiac death.*

So a heart attack is a heart muscle problem. Sudden cardiac death is what they call an electrical problem. The difference between various heart disease conditions was seen when actresses Debbie Reynolds and Carrie Fisher, mother and daughter, tragically died within a day of each other in December 2016. Carrie Fisher had a fatal massive heart attack; Debbie Reynolds died of a stroke the day after learning her daughter had passed away. Even medical experts agreed that Ms. Reynolds appeared to have died of a broken heart. In reporting on the two deaths, the *Hollywood Reporter*, a respected film-industry magazine, noted that there is actually a condition called "broken-heart syndrome," also known as "stress-induced cardiomyopathy."* The magazine quoted Dr. Mark Creager, director of the Dartmouth-Hitchcock Heart and Vascular Center and the past president of the American Heart Association. Broken-heart syndrome "is used to explain a very real phenomenon that does occur in patients who have been exposed to sudden emotional stress or extremely devastating circumstances," Creager said.*

EMERGENCY RESPONSE AT CHURCH

Sudden cardiac death, the malady that hit me, strikes without warning. I collapsed with no pulse, no consciousness, and no breathing. I have a medical team at the church that is ready to respond to an emergency in any of our services. The team members are professionals who are at least registered nurses, and the team also includes a few physicians. They immediately came forward and started giving me CPR. One of those trained women brought me back. Then they called EMS.

The funny—and telling—thing was that I woke up giving orders. I opened my eyes and said to the people attending me, "Hey, you guys, get away from me. Move back—I'm getting too hot!"

The EMS team arrived, strapped me up, and proceeded to carry me out on a stretcher. Before, during, and after this traumatic event, I felt no physical symptoms. I had no chest pains, no headache, no sweating, and no tingling up and down my arm—none of that. Later, my chest was extremely sore from the vigorous pressure that my church medical team had applied to bring me back.

Needless to say, the congregation was in pandemonium. A cacophony of prayer bombarded heaven on my behalf. People were shocked, trying to see and figure out what had happened, and they were understandably concerned about my condition. As the paramedics carried me out of the building, I waved my hand to let the congregation know I was okay. I recognize now that I was still trying to direct things and show a degree of control—despite having literally died and been brought back just a few minutes before.

In the ambulance, the paramedics ran an electrocardiogram (EKG) on me—a quick measurement of the heart's electrical activity—that showed I had suffered no damage to my heart. At the hospital, the medical team had no real explanation for the disruption. I did not actually suffer a heart attack, which involves damage to part of the heart due to lack of oxygen, usually caused by a blocked artery. My heart just stopped! The doctors inserted stents into my chest cavity, which are tubes that widen the valves that enter and leave the heart, but this was just as a precaution.

For the following five months, and for twenty-four hours each day, I wore a life vest that was really a portable defibrillator. The medical professionals treating me did several tests on my heart and circulatory system during that time, and they found nothing wrong. So when I say God made me lie down, I mean that I see this traumatic experience as primarily a tremendous wake-up call. It proved to me that I needed to make major changes in my work habits and lifestyle if I wanted to keep living—and become more effective, not just busier.

Too Busy

I was due for a change. I had to reflect back in my own mind: *How did I get to this place where God had to make me lie down?* I realized that for too long I had been trying to do everything for everybody, never saying no. I had been constantly taking two engagements at the same time and making both of them.

When I was twenty-one years old, I became the pastor of Second Ebenezer in December 1976. I assumed control of a church that had only sixty-six members and had missed its last thirty-one bank payments. I worked as a bank teller until the congregation grew to the point where I could focus on the church full time. By 2016, when I was approaching my fortieth year as pastor, the church had become a five-thousand-member church with fifty distinct ministries. We completed our current worship center, which has a sanctuary with over three thousand seats, in October 2007, with a development cost of $25 million—just into the Great Recession. In addition, another $65 million was invested by Vanguard Community Development Corporation, the development arm of our ministry. Surviving that downturn, when many families left the city of Detroit, was the toughest test of my ministry. The City of Detroit suffered the largest municipal bankruptcy in US history. Our largest employers, General Motors and Chrysler, also went bankrupt. Our church built a worship center and developed affordable housing in the middle of the recession, in a bankrupt city.

For nearly thirty years of my forty years at the church, I worked seven days a week without a day off. I kept that schedule because I work weekends—Saturday is for weddings, funerals, and other events. Of course, Sunday is also an all-day workday. The day that I would need to take off should be either Monday or Friday—but I very rarely took off Monday or Friday. I'm involved in so many community activities, and I'm on so many boards. I've done that kind of stuff for *years*—all of my life. I've begun to realize that my motivation for doing so much goes back to my childhood, but we'll get to that later.

Suffice it to say that because of my longtime approach to my goals and accomplishments, I adopted a stubborn mind-set: *If I don't, it won't!* That is, the job won't get done unless I do it! It is so often the mantra with people who see themselves as high achievers. If I need you to do something, if I ask you to do it, and even if I *pay* you to do it, I'm still going to do the job my way, myself. Because you're never going to do what I need you to do, especially not the way I need you to do it. In the end, if I really need something to get done, "if I don't, it won't."

I have also come up with the term *work martyrdom*. It's when a person like me approaches his or her job with this kind of mind-set: "I'm really a martyr, because everybody doesn't have my work ethic here. I fill in the gaps. Why? Because I'm talented, I'm gifted, I'm a multitasker, I'm an overachiever, and I'm a workaholic. Whatever you want to call me, good or bad, I know I have what it takes to fill in the gap."

According to a June 2016 report by the US Travel Association's Project: Time Off, 55 percent of American workers did not take all of their vacation days in 2015, up from 42 percent in 2013.* I certainly didn't for the first twenty-five years of my career. I would tack on a day or so to a convention or a conference and call that a vacation. If I was going to some national or regional meeting, I would designate one extra day as a rest day while I was gone; but otherwise, I'd be working really hard at a convention. In many instances, at the convention, I wasn't just there in the seats; I had some role—fulfilling some responsibility or obligation. At many of the religious conventions I attended, I also served as a musician. So they wanted me to be there when the event started in the morning. I didn't necessarily have to be there at the 7:30 a.m. session, but I got up anyway! I'd be there all day, and I also played music at the night sessions. Later on, when I got involved as an officer on an administrative level, it became my *responsibility* to be there for many additional sessions. So there I'd be at a conference, away from home, putting in a twelve-hour day of activity. If the conference ended on a Thursday, I'd stick around for my extra day of rest on Friday, then come back on Saturday. But let's be honest: that's no vacation!

One other thing I have to mention is my habit of always returning from out of town for my weekend services as church pastor. I don't know when I have ever, except for sickness, taken off two Sundays in a row. The prevailing travel church culture in my community was never to miss a Sunday, if possible. When I traveled globally—to hold a crusade in Africa, for instance—I would leave on Sunday night or Monday morning, miss one weekend, but be back by the following weekend. Even after my own wedding on a Saturday, I was in church the next day—then left for our honeymoon on Sunday night. At the time, I thought it was quite noble!

Obviously, I was pushing too hard. Little wonder that I was *made* to lie down.

ATTACKED BY THE DEVIL?

When you have a life-threatening sudden-death experience and you return from that, you naturally wonder why it happened. You try to make sense of it, especially if you live a life of faith and believe that you are protected by and guided by a loving God.

I don't have the mind of God, so I cannot explain with full certainty what God did or what God allowed when I suffered sudden-death syndrome during a New Year's Eve church service. It would be presumptive of me to say, "I know this was God's plan," or "I know it was the devil." I could find examples to prove either explanation.

One school of theological thought would say, "The enemy did this. I was attacked by an evil spirit." If I were in a church testimony service, I would get a lot of shouts and a lot of approval if I described my experience as a case of having been attacked by the devil—as I did the Lord's work right in church. "I cheated death!" I could declare, and that is literally the truth. I did.

Yet, as I see it, I was not simply blindsided by a spiritual attack. When I look at the facts, I can plainly say that at the time I was overworked. I was the one who burned myself out. I was the one who made poor choices. I was the one who ran myself ragged.

As I prayed and reflected on my physical setback, the revelation I got from God about my situation was that God really did it for me, more than the devil doing it against me. God literally made me lie down—as described in Psalm 23:2.

A CLOSER LOOK AT PSALM 23:2

When you do an exegetical study of the Twenty-Third Psalm, you will discover that the concept of being made to lie down is more comforting than originally thought.

Being made to do anything is counterintuitive to the nature of humanity. Nobody wants to be made to do anything. A baby instinctively does not want to be told what to do. Babies will quickly rebel if you seek to make them comply with anything they don't want to do. We were given free moral agency for a purpose. So if God made me lie down as the result of the medical emergency I survived, I might naturally wonder if I was being reprimanded for being out of God's will.

Well, what you find in the original Hebrew language is a concept of the shepherd causing a sheep to lie down and lean against him. He doesn't walk away with a trite or dismissive "I hope you feel better." Instead, the Great Shepherd that David describes in the psalm lies down next to the sheep. He comforts and encourages his sheep, and holds it firmly but gently, expressing secure and protective love, with no hurry and no rush involved.

"He maketh me lie down" does not mean abandonment. Nor does it mean that being made to lie down is a punishment. It is actually a comfort, because the shepherd is there, allowing the sheep to rest and lean against him. The reliance of the sheep is no longer upon itself, but upon a trustworthy shepherd who is able to shield the sheep from hurt, harm, and danger.

So being made to lie down was not a punishment to me. It was not putting me in the penalty box, to use an ice hockey analogy. There was reason and purpose behind it. This is the second school of thought that would be invoked in any theological discussion of my medical emergency. It was really for my own good. It was a matter of Him giving me the opportunity to lie down and lean against Him, to recognize that my true strength comes from Him and not from me. I no longer had to depend just on me to accomplish all of the things I had been trying to do. My ailment and convalescence was for my good.

I believe that while God saw that all of the work that I've done is great stuff, and that I've accomplished much, if He had not allowed the physical emergency where I was made to lie down, I would have never sat down on my own. I would have kept doing everything I was doing. I would never have leaned in the way that I'm leaning now.

I prefer to say that God did for me what a shepherd would do for a sheep that is weary, that is worn, that is depleted, and that needs to be replenished. It makes sense that a good shepherd would make such a weary sheep lie down, and then make that sheep lean on him. God really laid me down so that I had to lean on Him in a way that I've never done before. I finally got a chance to rest. So the experience was for my good. And I'm being forced to live afterward in a way that I've never done before, because I've never tried before to put this much balance into my life.

EDUCATING OTHERS ABOUT HEART DISEASE

One of my responses to my crisis has been to try to warn others to avoid what I experienced. I lent my voice and political support to the American Heart Association's campaign to get the Michigan legislature to require all students to be taught hands-only CPR before graduation from high school. The heart association initiated legislation to this effect in mid-2015, and lobbied state lawmakers until its passage in December 2016. I shared my personal story with legislators and at public meetings, urging that this common-sense measure become law. Therefore I was proud to be a guest at the formal signing of the bill into law by Michigan's lieutenant governor Brian Calley on December 28, 2016. Michigan became the thirty-sixth state to approve the hands-only CPR requirement, which will be effective as of September 2017.

Cardiovascular disease is the number one killer in the world, accounting for 17.3 million deaths a year, according to the American Heart Association. That total is expected to reach 23.6 million deaths per year by the year 2030, the association estimates.* We should certainly do everything we can to get those numbers down, and most importantly, to avoid adding to those grim and tragic statistics.

CHAPTER 2

THE HIGH COST OF STRESS, OVERWORK, AND BURNOUT

We live in an increasingly stressful society for many reasons. The fast pace, competitiveness, and demanding nature of the modern global economy and the information-based workplace is a primary source of stress. Beyond the world of work, you see additional complexity everywhere you look. You see division. You see disharmony. You see conflict. You see people at odds with one another. And you see our differences being pointed out and emphasized.

SOCIAL COMPLEXITY ADDS STRESS

Those things that are at the heart of conflict between people are increasingly becoming underscored and even celebrated. It becomes not a matter of honoring and celebrating our diversity, but rather celebrating division. It is the celebration of disengagement. Everybody's angry. I don't care if you're a Democrat or a Republican, if you're white, black, or Hispanic—whoever you are—everybody's mad about something. We don't live in a world of harmony. Never had that been clearer than it was in the aftermath of the divisive and chaotic US presidential election of 2016.

The challenge becomes reconciling the diverse, unrealizable, and unattainable expectations that everybody has. Everyone wants to defend their rights. And to be perfectly honest, that social impulse came directly from the American civil rights movement of the 1950s and '60s. Once black people proved that they could successfully press for equal opportunity, many other groups began to press their grievances in order to "get theirs." In our grievance-based society, everybody now says, "I have a right to this; I have a right to that." More often, we are seeing those who belong to groups that have traditionally had most of the advantages in the process of fighting to preserve their traditions and their control.

Most political observers of the 2016 US presidential election and the fractious first half year of the Trump administration agree that divisions in the federal government along party lines and the lack of bipartisan cooperation in the Congress rival some of the worst periods in American history. Such gridlock in Washington reflects social conflict across the country along racial, cultural, and economic lines that is as bad as what the nation experienced in the 1960s. Certainly leaders who can promote better communication, greater tolerance of others, and national unity are needed more than ever.

OVERWORK CREATES STRESS AND ITS CONSEQUENCES

The late twentieth century produced more demands on every industry for greater productivity in the face of a growing global economy. Since then, our jobs and entrepreneurial ventures have expected more of each of us. Wages have been largely stagnant (except at the very top), but pressure on managers and "line" workers has increased. We're no longer leaving the job at 5:00 p.m. and coming back tomorrow to start all over again. The 9-to-5 schedule we used to call "the workday" is just a foundation, because there's a good chance that I will need to research or finish a report after I get home.

The job becomes so demanding that work becomes almost a 24/7 existence, to the extent that you don't even have to be in the office. Whoever thought that you wouldn't have to go to an office or a factory but that you'd work just as hard from home? "I work from home," some people brag, but they face the same performance demands, despite their flexibility. They don't have to rush to work, but they were up past midnight!

Economists and sociologists tell us that for decades, American workers have put in more hours on the job than workers in any other industrialized nation. A 2015 Gallup poll revealed that the average US employee worked 47 hours a week, or 2,370 hours a year.* Back in 1997, American workers were on the job only 2,000 hours a year—and that was still by far the most in the world.* The hours we have added to our work lives since then amounts to an increase of 10 weeks of work.*

The result is greater work-related stress. But stress and work are not a good match. A 2013 Kansas State University study found that people who work more than fifty hours a week suffer from poorer physical health—due largely to skipped meals—as well as poorer mental health, evidenced by depression.*

The *American Journal of Industrial Medicine* reported in 2014 that 18 percent of American workers put in sixty or more hours per week, a number that increases the likelihood of heart disease by 42 percent over those who work thirty-one to sixty hours a week.* Those who work eighty or more hours a week run a 94 percent greater risk of heart disease than those who work thirty-one to sixty hours, according to a study reported by the journal.* But also troubling is that the same study showed that those who worked thirty hours or less a week also had higher rates of heart trouble than those who worked thirty-one to sixty hours.* This suggests that part-time workers have similar stress rates as those who are overworked, perhaps because of worries related to the kind of work they do.*

An article in the *Atlantic* magazine cited a 2015 report produced by the business schools of Harvard University and Stanford University that studied the connection between mortality and ten common sources of workplace-related stress. The stress sources included long working hours and the lack of health insurance, for instance. The study found that 120,000 Americans die each year from health problems tied to job stress, such as cardiovascular disease, mental problems, and high blood pressure. In other words, stressing over the job leads to health problems "more deadly than diabetes, Alzheimer's or influenza."* The same study found that the financial cost of health problems connected to job-related stress could be 5 to 8 percent of America's annual health-care costs, or $180 million.*

The *Atlantic* article, entitled "The Alarming Long-Term Consequences of Workplace Stress," also referred to a 2005 study produced by Boston University's Sloan Work and Family Network that suggested workplace injuries occur more when people feel overworked. Workers who said they felt stressed from excessive work were also "20 percent more likely to say that they made lots of mistakes on the job," according to the Sloan Work and Family Network report.* That report also found that generally bad health and bad habits like smoking were more likely with long hours and with shift work.* Betty Purkey, manager of Work/Life Strategies at Texas Instruments, was quoted in the Sloan report as follows:

> While we normally equate long hours at work with commitment, long hours are actually much more strongly correlated with increased risk for burnout—and burnout brings with it increased medical costs and lost productivity. Overwork may lead to short-term business gains but often at huge costs both to the corporation and to the individual. Looking for ways to improve efficiency and effectiveness both at the company and the team level can help reduce overwork.*

The authors of the Harvard–Stanford report on overwork suggested that employers should encourage company-wide events, increase mentoring, and do more to keep employees for the long term rather than the short term, according to the *Atlantic* article.* In the end, any steps to reduce stress at work would be beneficial to the health of workers, the Harvard–Stanford authors wrote. "Even though it is likely that these stressors cannot be completely eradicated in practice, our analysis suggests that even reducing their prevalence could potentially go a long way in improving health outcomes and cost."*

WHEN STRESS COMES WITH THE JOB

The stress we experience used to be mainly on the body. But we've transferred much of it to the mind. A man who used to work at Ford

Motor Company's foundry in Dearborn, Michigan, would come out of there at the end of the day full of smoke, maybe with harmful materials in his lungs, but without as much mental or emotional fatigue as someone who works in a Ford office today. I may have on nice clothes and work in a nice environment, but I'm under pressure to be precise, to solve problems, to meet a deadline. I have to know what I'm doing at all times or else lose face in a competitive environment where if I don't cut the mustard, I'm out.

Adding to vocational stress is the fact that too many workers aren't doing work they enjoy. The motivational speaker Les Brown has noted that 86 percent of people work at jobs they hate.* We live in an environment where they pay you just enough to keep you from quitting. And you work just hard enough to keep from getting fired. I've heard it said "most people are not happy; they're just not unhappy enough to do anything about it." How many people are literally unhappy with what they do? How many people are looking at their lives and seeing that they've never been able to have a job or a vocation where they were literally doing something that they felt called to do, that they felt comfortable doing, that they derived joy and fulfillment from doing? Doing what one dislikes or even hates each day adds to the stress and the imbalance in a person's life. When you're on that kind of job, your entire life can be one of survival from one paycheck to the next. It's "I need a job, I don't need a career. I just need something to take care of my immediate needs." It's really about survival mode.

Other folks choose honorable careers that are stressful by definition. For instance, many people choose a career course that includes military service. They do their service and then come back home. The next step for many is to get into law enforcement. So the public controversies we've seen in recent years is related, I'm sure, to the stress that law enforcement officers and other first responders live with. I'm sure that the past trauma of working or fighting in a war zone has an impact on the psyche of a person in this line of work. When you look at police officers in New York, or LA, or Detroit, you can see that they're not just cops. They are trained to use violence, when necessary, to stop violence. But they are also required to be peacekeepers, negotiators, diplomats, and lifesavers. Likewise, firefighters are not just putting out fires! They are living a lifestyle that really holds the line for the rest of our society. Even a fulfilling job requires that a person find balance by discovering ways to deal consistently with stressful situations.

Stress can be present even if it looks like nobody's working. You know, if you're from the Midwest or back East and you go to Los Angeles, California, it looks like everybody is all la-la-la, having fun all the time. In the middle of the day, the traffic is jammed. If you're visiting, you might ask yourself, *Where is everybody going? Are they working? It looks like everybody's having lunch!* They appear to relaxing and having a good time, whether at the spa, on the beach, or wherever! You might look around and ask, *What in the world do people do here?*

Yet even in an environment that appears to be more relaxed and more accepting of a recreational approach to living, expectations in LA are so high that many people end up on drugs—and some end up committing suicide. Those people can't deal with the stress.

STRETCHED AND STRESSED IN EVERY AREA OF LIFE

Society's demands on all of us continue to increase. There used to be a time when people came out of high school, went to college, then got married and started a career. They did all these things in sequence. Now, if you desire to do well, even while you're married and you've got kids, you're working a full-time job and you're going to school. Maybe you volunteer for extra overtime, maybe you're working a little side job, maybe you've even got a little business on the side. I mean, that's life for many, many people now. It's not a matter of living one season of life at a time, in sequence. We're living life with everything in the pot stirred up. We are led to believe that this level of hyperactivity points us to success.

But to be perfectly honest, too many people are frustrated by the fact that with all of the personal sacrifices they make, and all of the time they spend on tasks beyond their jobs, they're still stressed out. They're burnt out, but not necessarily any more successful. Some break through and reach a higher standard of living—but for most, it takes everything they're doing just to survive, just to pay the house note, pay the car note, and send the kids to college.

This is why overwork and subsequent burnout are at epidemic rates.

Adults are doing more, kids are doing more, and the family is doing more. We're "on" all of the time. We're connected at all times. Current culture in America and elsewhere pushes us to work, not rest, even during recreational pursuits. Talk to the average person; there's no such thing as spare time. People used to say, "Well, in my spare time, I play checkers or whatever." Today, nobody's got time to play checkers. We hardly give ourselves any spare time. The entertainment industry is growing faster than ever, but everything we do, even have fun, seems to fit into a highly structured routine. Take working out, for example. What people used to do is just get up every morning and do some calisthenics or take a walk—"my morning constitutional," they called it. Get up and eat a banana or an apple, drink some water, then walk down the block and walk on back. That was good. But now, even exercise is stressful. You've got people picking up truck tires and throwing them around. You've got to go to the gym and meet your trainer. It's just like having a teacher. This is beyond calisthenics. This ain't jumping jacks—it's real work!

Everything that we're doing now seems more advanced and complex than it used to be—certainly beyond what it strictly has to be. We do have tools to help make some things easier. But all of that technology often makes things harder, it seems. Cable TV and cell phones used to be entertaining conveniences, welcome enhancements that we could take or leave. But smartphones and niche networks—with unique programs that are broadcast on television as well as online—are increasingly seen by many of us as life essentials, true necessities that we can't do without! I might open my email inbox and see three hundred or four hundred messages received. Somehow I've got to get through all of that, even if it's just to delete them. Does the latest high-tech function make life more convenient? I think it accelerates the pace. Now that brings a sense of convenience, but it also brings added stress.

If you go into any bookstore or search any newsstand, you'll find that every self-help book and magazine is going to be showing you Seven Ways to Success, or Ten Ways to Be Better, or Five Ways to Think Outside the Box. It's going to be getting you to do more. You've got to spend more time, become more efficient, interact with others more. Everybody says "more!"

Whether Good or Bad, Stress Puts Us in Fight Mode

Stress is often exacerbated by the momentum of career advancement and business growth. Taking full advantage of an opportunity to do what you love, what brings you fulfillment, is a different kind of challenge. It can add what seems to be "good stress" to your life. The gray area between good stress and bad stress is often like good cholesterol versus bad cholesterol—virtually indecipherable. The late Detroit mayor Coleman Young often said that even racism is like high blood pressure: you can have it and not know it. How many millions of people have diabetes, HIV, heart issues, or the onset of dementia and don't know? Life inevitably brings you to places, junctures, crossroads, even distractions that are often indecipherable. Which means that sometimes you're hitting these leverage points, these certain punctuation points in your life, and you're not even aware of it because you're so busy and so consumed, not comprehending that you might be reaching a dangerous threshold.

There is something in our human instinct that always wants more. You can see it in the smallest child. But we need parameters in our lives. We need boundaries. We need to understand the power of limitations. The Bible tells me that goodness and mercy are supposed to be following me (Psalm 23). Did I ever give them a chance to catch up? Or did I always outrun them with my busyness?

Whether the source of personal stress is a situation that we despise or one that means everything to us, allowing stress to build unaddressed and untreated too often means that something unhealthy can be lurking within us. It could be a disease—a sudden illness or a chronic condition—a proclivity, a tension, or an apprehension. It may be something unseen, asymptomatic, yet real. Our bodies do speak to us. The question is, do we listen? And what are the penalties if we ignore our bodies' signals?

If you ignore a stoplight, chances are high that you'll get in an accident. If you ignore your bills, you will find yourself with relinquished property and low credit scores. Similarly, our bodies give us signs and signals—and we cannot afford to ignore them.

One of my children once dropped a bottle of Vernors ginger ale, a drink that has traditionally been more highly carbonated and stronger in flavor than the average soda pop. (Detroiters who remember when the Vernors company headquarters and main bottling plant was in midtown Detroit will tell you that the flavor and carbonation used to be even more intense.) Well, my kids picked up the dropped bottle quickly—and twisted the cap open before I could stop them. The next thing I knew, foam was shooting from the bottle all over the room. It was impossible to put that powerful stream back—and it produced a sticky mess everywhere.

That situation reminds me of poor health, aggravated by habits like worry, overwork, and bad diet. When we're overloaded, when we've passed capacity, the problem sort of shoots out unexpectedly, like the soda pop from that bottle. It shoots out and we end up wasting a whole lot. We lose a lot of momentum. We can't put what we've lost back in the bottle. That's what life is like sometimes. Whatever you waste now, you'll want later. There will be a demand for it that you won't be able to fulfill.

Medical specialists tell us that stress puts our bodies in "fight mode"—a position that is both offensive and defensive—in order to keep us safe in times of danger. The following is according to Dr. Isaac Eliaz, a physician who attempts to integrate natural remedies and common sense into medical care:

> During periods of high stress, certain chemicals within the brain, including the neurotransmitters dopamine, epinephrine and norepinephrine, begin to rise, causing larger amounts of these and other "fight-or-flight" hormones such as adrenalin to be released by the adrenal glands. The release of these chemicals contributes to certain physiological effects, including rapid heart rate, higher blood pressure, and a weakened immune system.*

Eliaz notes that "even if it seems we're building a tolerance to stress, our nervous system is still dealing with an overload which can seriously affect overall health in the long run."* He and other medical professionals tell us that the negative physical effects of prolonged stress include heart disease, cancer, high blood pressure, and ulcers. Other side effects include poor digestion, and tensed muscles, which can lead to severe headaches.*

Meanwhile, the mental and emotional effects of stress can produce depression, anxiety, inability to focus or reason well, frustration, anger, and relationship problems, according to Eliaz.*

Stress has become something that is very difficult for us to deal with. We need strategies that integrate work and our personal lives. We need strategies to help us remain effective, efficient, and productive in the face of an increasingly stressful world.

CHAPTER 3

DRIVEN TO WIN IN A STRESSFUL CITY

A Pastor's Search for Work-Life Integration

Let me introduce you to my profession. I'm a church pastor. Plenty of people believe mine is the softest of the soft professions, so easy that charlatans are attracted to it —because the money is supposedly so easy to make. I can assure you that the challenges of my job are tremendous, and the pressure and stress is sky-high, every day!

Ask yourself, if you had the opportunity, would you do it?

Pastors have a hard time finding balance. Being a pastor is not a switch that turns on and off. You are basically on all of the time. That makes it sometimes hard to interact well. It is hard to even make friends when you are a pastor, because when people find out who you are, they revert to their religious or antireligious alter egos. I've been on a plane and sat next to many a person who will ask me, "Well, what do you do?" If I say, "I'm a minster," the conversation automatically changes to something tense and unnatural.

"You're a minister … Wow … So, like, do you have a church? Your own church?" That's the first thing people ask.

"Yes, I do."

"You're in charge of it?"

"Yeah."

"Well, how big is it?"

"I don't know; five, six thousand people, I guess."

"And you do that yourself?"

It's like this incredible profession I'm part of—and I know that there is a lack of understanding about it.

But some people will come up with a patronizing kind of response. "You know, my great-grandmother was really dedicated to church. She used to give a missionary offering all of the time to try and help kids over in Africa." Or, "We had one of the missionaries come to our home once, and boy, that was a great experience!" And I'm never surprised to have someone bring up how much they love the exuberant church choirs they've heard. It's a matter of trying to be friendly and find common ground, to be sure, but it comes across as placating a religious person who is "different."

It got to the point where I would truthfully tell people who asked, "I'm a developer. I do community development. I build housing." The typical reply would then be, "Oh, really!" And we'd have a regular conversation, a business conversation. It would be an "I'm okay, you're okay" kind of conversation. If I should say, "I work for IBM," then the average person would ask, "Oh, yeah, well what do you do there?"

"Well, you know, I'm on the road. I'm a sales guy."

"Oh, okay, great. That's cool. How 'bout them Tigers? How 'bout that World Series with Cleveland and the Cubs?" In other words, the reaction would be, "You're cool; you're normal."

But when you identify yourself as a religious leader, that's when the guards come up. The pseudopoliteness comes up. Most people shun religious and political conversations, because normally those generate high emotions or strong disagreements, and not many people want that. It's as if I'm not allowed to be like normal folks. I mean, I brush my teeth, I drink Coca-Cola, I eat cornflakes and fried chicken like everybody else. But I'm seen as someone who doesn't do all of that because I'm "religious."

So I've found that pastors, or religious workers and leaders, experience an added level of stress socially. Those of us who are in the business of helping others are not immune to the impact of that kind of stress. The number of pastors who have mental illnesses and need counseling themselves is huge, an ever growing problem. We even see an increase in suicide among pastors, as hard as that may be to believe. No one is saying too much about any of these problems, but we need to deal with them.

A person has to assess what level of stress they're at, first of all, so that they know what kind of solutions they need to employ. As urban pastors and ministers learn to focus and prioritize more effectively, we might become examples to those in other industries and professions. Right now, urban ministers could stand to take a page from the specialists we see in professional football and professional baseball. Football has punters and field goal kickers who become experts in kicking an oval pigskin just the right way, using just the right velocity, to make it land where it should. Baseball has starting pitchers and relief pitchers who are experts at gripping the ball and throwing it at the right speed to get batters out at critical points in the game.

Whether you are a preacher, an engineer, an artist, a businessperson, or a single mom—all of us need to determine what we are best able to do, and then do that well!

A Leader Should Not Be a Beast of Burden

The stress that I have experienced for most of my professional life has been the stress of leadership. The sphere of leadership in the black community—in religious circles, civil rights circles, even business circles—has always been a bit lopsided. By that, I mean that it is personality driven.

The black businesses that the public knows as the most prominent and most successful are led by larger-than-life personalities. The same is true with civil rights organizations. Most people don't know anything about the Southern Christian Leadership Conference. They know something about Martin Luther King, though, because he was so much bigger than the organization. I come from a culture where personalities are often bigger than organizations. I agree with those who say that this cultural viewpoint is lopsided, not the way things should be. But, generally speaking, it is how most things in my community have been structured and organized historically. People who join and support our organizations—and that includes our churches, in many instances—are comfortable with groups dominated by one personality.

But often, the big questions are: What happens after? Where is the succession plan? And is that plan going to work? Are people going to receive and get behind the successor?

I've looked with great admiration at other cultures where things appear to work very smoothly. In corporate America, for example, most companies already have a CEO in mind if their current CEO unexpectedly needs to be replaced. They already know who the next chairperson or president will be. They have a succession plan in place that goes out a certain number of years. So they already know what to expect and whom to expect. And even if something happened to *that* person, they know who the next person in line would be. This is the kind of internal culture that exists within multibillion-dollar, sometimes international corporations. The corporation merrily moves forward, so to speak.

But when organizations and infrastructure are personality driven, as is the case so often in African American culture, that fact creates another weight on the shoulders of those of us who achieve. I find that sometimes the achievement involves reaching the point of being *larger than life*—so that you can pull the organization behind you, using your persuasive skills and the force of your personality. The alternative, which is certainly more attractive, is getting in front of an organization that's already moving and leading it.

Too many times, our organizations are wagons that we have attached to us, and we as leaders are the horse that has to make the wagon roll! The horse uses its energy and its strength, and eventually develops almost supernatural strength, constantly pulling a wagon full of people or products. Too often, leadership feels and looks like the relationship between a horse and a wagon.

But a horse attached to a wagon is not really a leader. That horse is a hired hand. That horse is a beast of burden! For many leaders of organizations, that's what our role has become. The same is true for people who are the caretakers in their families. They've turned into horses!

A workhorse not only labors around the clock but also doesn't even have time to relieve himself properly. Whether it's the field or the street, he's got to relieve himself on the job, wherever that might be. He doesn't even have a moment to seek his own privacy!

Oftentimes in life, this is what overachievers are doing. They're bulked up, they're extra strong, they have massive passion, and they have massive strength, unusual determination, and unusual drive. Those are the kinds of horses that are used. They're not show horses, they're workhorses! They're used to pull heavy loads. "We've got a big job for you!" people will tell a workhorse. You can bet they do!

Such service does have its rewards: the horse gets fed and the horse gets stroked. But the horse also gets whipped! After so many years of that, taking on the role of a horse, it weighs on you.

The Detroit Regional Chamber sponsors an annual policy conference each spring on Mackinac Island, a scenic northern Michigan resort situated between the Great Lakes Michigan and Huron. Motorized vehicles are not allowed on Mackinac Island; the only modes of travel or transport are either bicycles or vehicles powered by horse. Participants in the annual conference ride around in horse-drawn carriages. I have attended the Mackinac conference many times, and when I recall how we get on those carriages and wait for the horses to pull away, I think of how ten of us will be sitting there in one of the quaint wooden carriages, laughing and talking. There will be plenty of luggage on the back, or some other kind of cargo. But we give little thought to the poor horse we are about to put to work. We just ask, "Why isn't the horse moving?" and say, "Let's get going!"

But sometimes the horse gets tired. To most passengers, the horse's struggle doesn't matter—he just needs to keep moving. To be sure, the horse is massive! But he has to pull ten of us, with luggage, up a steep hill to the historic Grand Hotel. So many times the people take the horse for granted, enjoying the ride, but not realizing the strength the horse is providing.

To bring this analogy back to the struggles that human leaders experience, my point is that a leader should not be a "horse" as he or she leads an organization. Rather, we leaders should be drum majors of a parade. A parade is different. Someone has to march up front, to give direction, but everyone is moving under their own power.

I was one of those people who was a workhorse in almost everything I've been involved in. Yes, I have had a great, great life of success, and I'm not ashamed to say that. I'm not ungrateful; I'm very appreciative of the success I've had. But after this experience, I began to assess: how many wagons was I pulling?

Yes, I've had a great life of success. Many times workhorses are successful in terms of what they've been able to pull. But it is the *wear and tear of the pull* that causes you to reprioritize and to balance out. You wouldn't have gotten where you've gotten had you not done what you've done. But it's the pull that exacts such a high price, a price that most people underestimate.

There is a certain kind of horse that is a show horse. Show horses are brought out and they prance around; they look pretty. "Oh, look at his mane, look at his coat. He's so spry; he has such energy," people say. Yeah, he's not pulling that wagon! Workhorses are made to pull the wagon. A show horse can attract attention and even enhance the image of an organization or product, but not even a show horse is an adequate leader.

MOTOR CITY, STRESSFUL CITY

Detroit is an iconic American city that is known around the world for industrial production, great music, and the toughness and resiliency of its people. I love my city. I've been blessed and fortunate here. I've had more than a modicum of success in my city. That comes as a surprise to some people who live elsewhere, because many view Detroit as the most stressed city in America. I have to reluctantly agree with that assessment, because of my experience and because there is research to support it. For example, a 2016 study by WalletHub.com compared stress levels across 150 US cities, using metrics from five major categories. The categories were as follows:

- Work-related stress
- Money-related stress
- Family-related stress
- Health- and safety-related stress
- [Success] Coping with stress

Based on those five particular metrics, Detroit was identified in this particular study as America's most stressed city.* Two key metrics that figured in Detroit's overall stress ranking were tied to money-related stress. Although the survey ranked Detroit fourteenth in the nation for stress related to money, Detroit's high poverty rate and its residents' low credit scores were the worst in the nation.* According to the US Census Bureau, 40 percent of Detroiters live below the poverty line, the highest percentage in America.* Meanwhile, the average credit score among Detroit residents was 590, at the very bottom nationally, according to TransUnion.* That's pretty deep.

Detroit also ranked as the city with the highest family-related stress in the nation, according to the WalletHub study, with its 41 percent divorce rate being the country's third worst, behind Cleveland, Ohio, and Birmingham, Alabama.* Finally, the way Detroit copes with stress was second worst in the country, the survey concluded. That is, Detroiters were less likely to see therapists or exercise, and more likely to smoke or drink, as they dealt with stress.*

So, although I live in a great city, a city that I love, a city where I've been blessed and fortunate, I have to acknowledge that I've found the stress level in my city to be higher than that in most other cities. I'm in a stressed environment, and that only exacerbates the big issue that I have begun to address: achieving a personal lifestyle that is less stressful and more balanced. Being part of a fundamentally stressful city will typically only make things worse.

Don't get me wrong, Detroit is a great city, in ways recognized only by those who spend time here, get past the stereotypes, and discover its assets. *But*—although a transformation of Detroit's downtown and midtown areas is under way, and although the city is becoming much more attractive, Detroit residents still live in an environment of stress. An environment of stress will lead you inevitably toward stress-related outcomes. One of my goals with *I Did It to Myself* is to help people who live in stressful kinds of environments to cope with them and to overcome them. The truth is that to a certain extent, all of us are living increasingly in a complex world. We are all living in stressful environments. There are expectations that enforce that.

Taking a biblical perspective, it is easy to relate to the prophet Isaiah, who said, "Woe is me … I'm a man of unclean lips, and I live among a people of unclean lips" (Isaiah 6:5). In other words, he was saying, "It's bad enough that I've got my own issues; my problem is that I'm in an environment where everybody has a similar affliction."

Therefore, someone who is serving others and trying to produce change in a stressful city has to be careful about maintaining his or her own spiritual, mental, and physical health. If the city is already stressed, then spinning plates and remaining calm under pressure becomes extra tough.

Precocious Child, Overachiever

How did I get to be who I am, and why do I do what I do?

Most of us have asked that question from time to time, and all of us should challenge ourselves with that kind of personal assessment.

I grew up in a great home, a religious home led by great parents. There were fairly strict standards. But we had a traditional black family, in my opinion. We weren't rich by any means. We did fairly well with rather humble means, but I didn't know how humble our circumstances were. I thought that life for our family was pretty good!

I was a precocious child. I guarantee that I'm not as smart today as I was as a kid. I got way ahead of myself. In school, I got great grades and was double promoted twice. I passed the admissions test and was accepted into Cranbrook, a very prestigious private school in suburban Detroit that counts Mitt Romney as one of its alumni. But my parents could not afford the Cranbrook tuition. There were no scholarships and no financial aid at the time. So I did not go to Cranbrook.

But I did outstanding things in a lot of different areas. I was always achieving. I was a bigtime spelling champion. I won the spelling bee for several years sponsored by the *Detroit News*. I was briefly a batboy for the Detroit Tigers, when legendary manager Charlie Dressen was there. (Dressen was managing the Brooklyn Dodgers when Bobby Thomson of the New York Giants hit the famous home run against them that won the pennant for the Giants in 1951.) My time with the Tigers was just for a summer, but it was an example of the very outstanding stuff I was doing as a little bitty kid and as a young adolescent. Then of course, in church I was a musician. I was a singer and I played piano and organ.

Success often takes curious paths. A seemingly unlikely confluence of circumstances often leads to the introduction or the door opening or a light bulb moment that brings one in alignment with purpose and greatness.

The late heavyweight champion Muhammad Ali got started as a boxer after someone stole his shiny new bicycle. At age twelve, he proudly pedaled off to a downtown exhibition in his hometown of Louisville, Kentucky. When the show was over, the bike was gone. In tears, young Cassius Clay sought out a policeman named Joe Martin. "If I find the kid who stole my bike," he said, "I'll whoop him."* And Martin told him that he'd better learn how to box before he went out looking for a fight. The police officer offered to let Cassius join the boxing class as he ran into the gym. He never got his bike back, but in six weeks, he got his first fight and whooped the guy.* That win propelled him to an amateur career that ended with an Olympic gold medal, and a professional career that made him arguably the greatest fighter of all time. Often, the pathway to success is filled with rather mundane clues of destiny and definition of direction. It is often uncanny how we seem providentially led in certain directions, through a confluence of circumstances that lead us to our destiny.

For me, it was a crib in the choir stand that was a precursor to the development of my musical talent and the achievements that I've since made in music. Likewise, the opportunities that I had to participate in stage plays, holiday speeches, spelling bees, recitals, and debate teams were all literally dress rehearsals for my destiny as a pastor and civic leader—forty years now of service ministry leadership that was built on a solid foundation. Don't ever despise small beginnings.

Yet whenever I did all of the things I accomplished as a child and a teenager—which I thought shook the world—my parents said, "That's nice, boy. Sounds good. All right now, go on upstairs now and clean up your room." I never felt a sense of celebration for the exceptional things that I was doing. I didn't expect a celebration for the mundane things, but for the exceptional things I did! My parents saw it differently, however. And my buttoned-down, highly disciplined father set the tone.

My dad was a pastor for more than fifty years. Our home was a very conservative traditional black Christian home. My father was a Methodist, a pastor in the historic African Methodist Episcopal denomination. AME congregations have sometimes been seen as highbrow, rather elitist people. AMEs have always had class; that's the image they carry. Their backs were a little stiffer; they've always had a lot of stature in and beyond America's black communities. The AME Church is where I received a tremendous spiritual and ethical foundation.

Dad would get up in the morning and put on a suit, even in the summertime. He wore a suit every day. He wore a suit around the house. Back then, many men wore short-sleeve dress shirts. Remember those? Dad would put on a short-sleeve dress shirt, a tie, and his suit pants or a pair of slacks. Believe it or not, he would cut the grass like that. My father didn't have casual clothes. So I grew up not having casual clothes. My dad had one of those big Royal typewriters. That's how he typed his sermons: one peck at a time, on a manual Royal typewriter. It was really something. He would sit there, wearing his dress shirt and slacks, and he'd type his sermon out. He was a pretty formal person. Dad was quieter and more reserved than I am—but powerful. I'd say he was a powerfully reserved sort of man.

But the nonchalance I received from my mom and dad, the people whom I wanted most to please, instilled in me a drive to be an overachiever, I believe. *I'm doing something, but I haven't done enough to impress them,* I told myself. *Let me go back and do something else spectacular.* Now, at least I wasn't going out and getting in trouble or stealing something for attention. I was never in danger of going to jail. But I would go out and seek to do something that I thought was *greater!* I wanted some greater achievement, so that maybe my parents would bring home a sack of cupcakes for me. Or maybe we'd have a special ice cream dessert some night—*something* that would happen to celebrate what I was accomplishing. I accomplished what I thought were exceptional things, but since for me exceptional was expected, nothing I did seemed to garner the sizzle I thought it deserved. That's what I believe drove me to be the overachiever I became.

When I reflected back in my own mind and asked myself, *How did I get to this place where God eventually made me lie down?*, the answer was clear: I'd gotten into the habit of doing everything for everybody, never saying no, never having the *ability*, it seemed, to say no. As a pastor and a community leader, I got used to accepting two engagements for the same exact time and making both events. I did that kind of stuff for *years.* All of my life I've done that. There's no doubt in my mind that I was *made* to lie down so that I might reflect upon the steps that high achievers and successful people need to take to make sure that they have balance in their lives.

Urban Ministry: Multidisciplinary Because of High Stress

So how can you be called to help hurting people without hurting yourself? There is undoubtedly going to be some hurt that comes back to you. There's going to be some stress that comes back to you. How can you be called to serve stressed people without absorbing some of that stress yourself?

The answer is that you really can't, not completely. As I've stepped back and taken a closer look at what I've been doing for four decades, and what many of my colleagues across America do every day, it has become obvious that an urban pastor is much more than a preacher. An urban pastor is a psychologist, a social worker, a philanthropist, a family counselor, and so much more. These are roles that a pastor in a stressful city, serving marginalized people, must adopt in order to be successful. More often than not, an urban pastor is going to be immersed in African American or Hispanic culture and will have likely personally experienced the additional stresses that racial or cultural discrimination place upon an entire community. Too often, hopelessness, poverty, poor education, lack of higher-educational opportunity, and mass incarceration all weigh heavily on the majority of an urban pastor's church members. All of these factors have a significant impact on what a pastor does if he or she is doing what one should be doing in an urban setting.

Our work is not just theological. It is not just motivational. It is not just inspirational. You find that you become multidisciplinary, multitalented, multifaceted. The necessity for being multidisciplinary is there. You will not be successful unless you are. Ministry is meeting needs, and the need in an urban ministry goes far beyond pie-in-the-sky "by and by when you die." It is "something sound on the ground while you're still around!"

So when you look at what we're called to do from a multidisciplinary standpoint, you see that the skill sets required for urban ministry are skill sets that almost no one else is required to have. Even the social worker in the urban setting can focus on functions with parameters, action easily recognized as "social work." But the urban pastor and the urban minister will take on an entire gamut of social ills and respond to those needs. Their success or failure is based on their ability to do so.

I'm not talking about black liberation, and I'm not talking black theology; I'm talking about black stress! In order to really minister to people in an urban setting, I'm expected to play a very broad range of roles. My members call me for legal advice because many of them can't afford a lawyer. They figure I know everything! They've seen me on TV next to leading officials and power brokers, so they think I know everything. I mean, my members call me and ask me whom they should vote for!

ARE YOU A 24/7 CRISIS MANAGER?

I have five thousand members in my church, and every parent used to ask me to come to their child's graduation. I was expected to sit at each ceremony for two or three hours, somewhere in the back, waiting for each child to walk across the stage. And I used to do it! I used to go. Afterward, I'd search for the family in a big crowd, hug the graduate, and tell them, "I'm so proud of you. God bless you." As much as I cared about each student, doing that was not a good use of my time. It was a bad trade-off. A much better approach is for me to invite the student into my office, hug on them, and talk to them about their educational experience. "Come on in here. Hey! How you doing? Tell me about it. How was the graduation?" That's what I do now. But back then, I would even agree to offer the prayer for the school's commencement invocation.

In addition, when somebody would die in the congregation, I used to go the funeral home with them and set up the arrangements. I would head down to the funeral home here in Detroit, holding my member's hand. I'd help them pick out a casket. Yes, I used to do all of that!

It was all about commitment, from my viewpoint. And what I found is, people will give you a whole lot of accolades for what you do for them that you don't have to do.

However, when you stop doing it, they may feel differently about you! "Oh, I don't know; he's way too busy," they might say. You encounter a user mentality in many low-income urban communities. I just think that mentality is a little higher when you have high levels of poverty. People are always looking for a hook-up, eager to attach themselves to somebody who knows somebody who knows somebody—because they never know when they're going to need something. To be frank, I've found that people come to pastors in the African American community for *everything!* To a certain extent, this is rooted in the traditional community leadership role that black pastors have had for more than 150 years in this nation. I tell my white pastor friends, "Nobody comes to you with anything! They might have a Bible question at most." But not too many people come to me with Bible questions. They rarely question what I teach from the Bible. They come to me when they can't pay their rent, when their electricity is cut off, even when they've got large bills that they want me to pay. Of course, the church can't respond to each individual emergency, but we do regularly support them. My point is that household crises are often the cry that I hear from my congregation. Not, "Show us Jesus! Let us see Jesus!" It is "Can you solve my problem, my crisis?"—and many people are *always* in crisis.

You and I Can Beat Our Job-Related Stress Challenges

It becomes easy to carry the burdens of work everywhere you go. You carry your work home and you carry life at home to work. To share just one of my experiences, my church built our current building in the middle of the economic downturn that became known as the Great Recession. We finished construction and moved into the building in 2007. Our operations and our prospects were headed straight up, and then all of a sudden, the Great Recession hit! Everything went to the bottom. Everybody lost jobs. And we lost six hundred families, who moved out of state. What I had to do, and the obligations we faced, were almost insurmountable. My wife helped me to manage it by providing some very needed components of leadership as a member of my staff. But as valuable as she was, full-time duty at the church just took too much life out of both of us! It was just overwhelming.

She became the "do you think?" person, my wife remembers. People came to her and asked her if she thought a certain solution to a certain problem was possible—before they tried to approach me. She was always the one whom everybody came to before they would come to me. She was the one who loved on everybody and listened to all their problems. She comforted people, which was a great need. But sometimes being the comforter is too much. It drains you.

Every pastor, everyone engaged in social outreach, deals with the complexities of involvement with the lives of others. But I've found that as I interact with my ministerial colleagues in the suburbs, some of them encourage their members to go home, love on their families, work hard, and be charitable—and that's about it. "See you next Sunday!"

By comparison, the multidisciplinary, pressure-packed nature of urban ministry has made many urban pastors stress experts. And I believe that the more stressful the situation or occupation that you find yourself in, the more you need to take the time to investigate ways to find the work-life integration that will help to balance your life.

I am determined to beat the work-related stress that I have battled for forty years. I've just recently begun to recognize what kind of pressure I was under. I've done my best to perform in that context. To see most of our people remain in the kinds of tough circumstances they've been in for four decades challenges me to improve what I do and how I think about my job. I've come to realize that I can be more effective by changing both my approach and my response to the congregation and community God has called me to teach and to serve. As we will see, you can make similar changes—and revolutionize your personal work-life integration.

CHAPTER 4

THE SEDUCTION OF BEING GIFTED

TALENTED, PASSIONATE, DISORGANIZED

Because high energy, highly talented people are not usually disciplined in the conventional way, they tend not to be as organized as others and do not follow the conventional path. They are driven by passion—something deep inside that motivates and drives them. Passion is the reason that they achieve at high levels. They are driven by instinct—as T. D. Jakes called it in his best-selling book by the same title.* What normally propels other people stifles high achievers. The standard protocol that other people use to reach their goals is not the way that gifted, talented, extraordinary people become high achievers.

Look at all of the successful people who dropped out of college, for example—many of them high-tech innovators. Bill Gates dropped out to launch Microsoft. Steve Jobs, the cofounder of Apple, was a dropout. Michael Dell of Dell Computers is a dropout. So is Larry Ellison of Oracle, and Travis Kalanick, the guy who started Uber, the transportation network. Mark Zuckerberg, who started Facebook, dropped out of Harvard. Jack Taylor, who started Enterprise Rent-A-Car, dropped out. So did Oprah Winfrey, who left Tennessee State University to focus on her first jobs in television.

Passion is very important. Think about the schools you attended growing up; it is more than likely that you can remember only a handful of your teachers. Which teachers do you remember? You remember the teachers that made an impact in your life. You don't necessarily remember the As, Bs, and Cs that they gave you. You remember that somehow their drive, their passion, their force of personality, or whatever it may have been made an indelible impact upon your life. Maybe you've had 150 teachers who led the classes that you've taken in your lifetime. But the four or five who stand out are the ones who had passion.

So passion is an undeniable element of success. Yet it is so important for gifted innovators to be able to prioritize, to rest, to integrate work and aspects of personal life—to ensure that their passion remains an attribute and doesn't become a problem.

ACHIEVERS ARE ALWAYS ENGAGED

God blesses you with influence. He gives you force and personality. He gives you a robust network of high-profile connections. He gives you the skill and ability to get things done. To bring people together. To make initiatives work. To drive innovation. To be an arbiter of ideas and to be a thought leader in the community. To help people to reach dreams, goals, aspirations, and ambitions.

I've identified with this image all of my life. I have enjoyed being a bold, exciting, ambitious, big-thinking, large-vision, change-the-world guy! But I've learned that you can be full of aspirational vision—as you are being labeled and criticized by others—and yet you can't find the on-ramps and the off-ramps and the rest areas in life.

When personal progress brings significant levels of stress to your life, you begin to ask yourself: Is busyness a good thing? Isn't it supposed to be admirable? I'm not supposed to be lazy, am I? Isn't being active all of the time a noble thing to do? Isn't this what it takes to get things done, in order to get ahead, to help change the world, and avoid being slothful? Then there's the scripture (Proverbs 6:6–8) that tells us to "go to the ant" and learn the value of industriousness.

GIFTED AND SEDUCED TO LIVE ON THE EDGE

Most gifted, high-energy people don't find average things to be hard to do. For instance, if you asked the average person to get up and speak in front of an audience, he or she would have difficulty. Studies have shown that one of the most stressful things in the world is to be a public speaker. So if I were to ask the average person to get up and speak before a church congregation or at a public meeting, it would be a horrifying experience! But if you were to ask me to do it, I would be already sitting there waiting for you to ask me. In fact, why haven't you asked me yet? Because I know I've got the skills. What do you need me to talk about? You don't even have to write it down; just tell me what it is! Because I'm gifted in that way. I'm talented. But my gifts bring me to a place where I can feel that I don't need discipline.

Similarly, I find that I often do my best work at the last minute. That might be part of my makeup. My ability to come through in the clutch generally does kick in when the pressure is on. If you, like me, can perform at that level, that's a good thing. It's very helpful. But you've got to be able to be disciplined enough to push yourself to perform.

Yet having the ability to deliver at the last minute or easily carry out tasks that others find difficult can ultimately be dangerous to your sense of perspective. I view the experience of performing under self-induced stress as a form of seduction—because if we are successful, it becomes exciting and intriguing for us to do things at the last minute all the time. It is literally seductive for you to be at a point where you thrive off stress. At that point, you earn bragging rights; you can say, "You know what? They just called me for that project. They called me Thursday and they needed it by Saturday. I knocked it out!" And it makes you feel like a hero. But eventually you find that you are succumbing to seduction and not a schedule.

The late Rod Temperton, who wrote several songs on the best-selling album of all time, Michael Jackson's *Thriller*, told the story of how he got a last-minute call from producer Quincy Jones the night before the legendary horror film star Vincent Price was scheduled to come to the studio and narrate the rap section of the title song. Quincy Jones had suddenly realized that Temperton should write out Price's part, rather than require the actor to walk in and try to make up "horror talk" on his own. Temperton agreed, but he forgot about the assignment until the next morning. At that point, he jumped in a cab and was forced to write Vincent Price's rap on the way to the recording studio. When he got to the studio, Vincent Price was arriving at the same time. Temperton ran into his office from the back door, gave what he had written to his assistant, and then ran to the front to meet Vincent Price. The assistant typed up the verses and had them ready when it was time for Price to step into the studio and record. Of course, the rest is music history.*

I do not deny that some of our finest moments have occurred and we've done some of our best work when we've completed a project impulsively, using adrenaline to meet the deadline. The problem is that if I've had two or three instances where I've stepped up and met the last-minute challenge, then I begin to believe that this is the way I can do it each time. That's part of the seduction.

I Did It to Myself is geared toward high-energy, high-profile, highly successful people from all walks of life. Those kinds of people have extraordinary gifts. And they are able many times to execute off schedule. However, they have been seduced if they are able to operate *off* schedule but are unable to do it *on* schedule. The seduction creates a pattern of doing *everything* off schedule. You see a lot of gifted and talented people living and working that way. Gifted people are often spontaneous about when they do things; for them, many times the rules don't apply. I particularly know musicians who fall victim of this seduction. They can be geniuses in terms of their music, but sometimes their lives are totally unbalanced and undisciplined because they have believed the seduction. They live their lives by it. But when you take creativity to an extreme and totally lose a sense of discipline, you begin to marginalize your effectiveness.

There needs to be a balance between the seduction of our gifts and the discipline of our schedules. We need to be able to know that we're balanced between the uninhibited seduction of the use of our gifts and the discipline of a scheduled life. At some point, we will overwhelm ourselves if we don't have this balance. Indeed, true success comes when we are able to strike a balance between the two. True success and apparent success are two different things. Some people have the trappings of success, but true success is a lifestyle. True success involves finding the sense of equilibrium that you need: emotional equilibrium, professional equilibrium, and your accomplishment equilibrium. You've got to find a balance for all of those things, and not everybody has the same balance. Gifted, successful people are those whose balance may be in a different place—but they still have to find it.

A musician may say, "Hey, look—I'm doing an all-nighter. I'm at the studio, I'm gonna be all night. We're gonna go all night till we get this done." An extremely organized person might say, "No, you're going to spend five hours at the studio, then you're going to eat dinner, and then you're going to rest. You can go back to the studio and start again tomorrow, early in the morning." But that's just not how gifted people work. They go when the spirit moves them. But balance would make them even better.

When Your Gift Does Not Produce Success

I've seen many gifted and talented people who are not successful. The question is, Why not? Maybe you've noticed that some of the best basketball players are guys who play in the alley and the park. The best players in the school are usually not on the team. So a lot of these gifted people never make it. And it's not because they don't have the talent. They don't have the discipline. They're not willing to pay the price. They're not willing to sacrifice. But sooner or later, sacrifices have to be made.

Many of them don't have a sense of appreciation for the advantages and opportunities they've been given. That's how being gifted and being smart can get in the way and be a stumbling block, believe it or not. Because another person who's not quite as gifted knows they've got to work at it. So guess what? They become committed to it and they work hard until they become better, better, better, better.

Some of the best preachers I know are not necessarily successful pastors or leaders. They've never reached a place that some would call success. Many of them are still pastoring in meager situations—but they're great preachers. Some are so much greater than the guy who's got the big church. In the same way, some top executives in a corporation—even the CEO—may not be the sharpest knife in the drawer. The CEO may have just gotten there because he played the political game in the corporation and treated everybody right and slapped everybody a high five at the right time. He moved up the ladder, and eventually there was nobody up there but him.

SKILLED PEOPLE LEARN TO REACT—AND DELIVER

I had to learn that *yes* is not my most powerful word. I learned this the hard way. We are acculturated to always deal with things in the affirmative. This means that if you are to be considered a good person, you don't turn down an opportunity to do something good. This attitude was part of the church culture in which I was raised. In the old-school church of my youth, it was not uncommon for a program to be under way and for the program emcee to announce, "We have a request for Sister Jackson to sing a solo." If you were Sister Jackson, it didn't matter that you were not on the program, had not been asked to perform, and were not prepared. If it were announced that "We have a request," then you had to get up there and do that solo! Sometimes the preacher himself would make the announcement. He would say, "Somebody requested Sister Jackson ... Come on up here, young lady!" And there you would go, walking up the stairs to the pulpit, shaking and unprepared. If they asked you to sing "something of your choice," you might not have anything on your mind. But once the request was made, there was no turning away. I can't remember ever being in a church service while I was growing up where someone made a request and the person requested didn't follow through. When you think about it, someone was forced to perform well when they had not been through the expected discipline such a task usually required.

I must admit that performing under such pressure made some of us who we are today. I learned how to swim because the swimming teacher literally threw me in the water. I never had formal lessons; I was never taught how to stroke and how to breathe in a class. I was in the ninth grade at Detroit's Mumford High School, a little bitty scrawny kid, and Coach Vaughn just threw me into the water—the *deep* water! That was because he knew that I was afraid of the water. All of a sudden, there I was in the deep end, doing my best to stay afloat. After I thrashed around for a while, Coach Vaughn extended a long bamboo stick toward me and pulled me out. My unexpected test happened in front of the whole class—not the way you'd prefer to face one of your biggest fears. But from that day on, I was determined to learn how to swim. Not only did I learn, but also I ended up on the swim team.

I'm just saying that we have been thrust into places, oftentimes, that we did not have preparation for or had not put any discipline into. We later found that we're most successful when we have a chance to prepare. You cannot predict, but you can prepare.

PLAYING LIFE BY EAR

Because gifted people don't operate in a routine manner, generally speaking, they don't plan as others do. Some fail to see the need to practice, because certain things come easier for them. We have a lot of schools of thought that suggest that you play to that strength. You know, use your gifts. Throw that schedule, that timetable, to the wind. Throw discipline to the wind, because it stifles your gift.

I've seen creative people lose their edge whenever they are not in the process of creating or performing. If a recording artist is not in the studio doing a new thing or on the road with tour dates, too often he or she will get off track. During the playing season, most athletes are disciplined. They work hard at practice. They go to bed on time. They eat decently and get their rest. They also spend extra time strengthening weak areas of their bodies or playing skills. But in the off-season, some gain extra weight. They might do a little drinking, a little smoking, a little this, a little that. They get way off the mark. Why? Because they're not in a disciplined environment. Former NFL quarterback Johnny Manziel was a prime recent example of an athlete who took his extraordinary talents for granted and was seduced into thinking he could slack off and still perform under pressure. He learned that he couldn't do that. His lack of focus, even though he was talented, cost him his career.

Athletes, musicians, and actors stay in the headlines for careless relationships and bad behavior when they are not in the process of doing the great work that made them famous—all because they have not submitted to a schedule of discipline. Too many lose their families and even their careers as a result. An actress who has been on top of the world, won awards, and been celebrated as one of the world's most beautiful women can suddenly find that the phone has stopped ringing and the movie roles have dried up.

Lower Standards Are Symptomatic of the Acceptance of Disorder

We're in a society now where our degree of appreciation is very different from what it used to be. Now, anybody can get a standing ovation at any time for anything. When I was a kid, that didn't happen. A standing ovation was reserved for something exceptional. Now, if a little kid gets up before an audience and doesn't say her speech properly, we give her a standing ovation anyway. If the preacher gets up and he's preaching but he isn't really saying anything, we'll still be standing up! Our adulation threshold is very low. We're not able to distinguish between what is exceptional and what is not. Anything that anybody does is okay now; it's good—as long as an individual had the nerve to do it. If the artist or performer says, "That's just me, and it's what I wanted to do, and that's who I am," today's audience will respond, "Well, congratulations! We appreciate you for just doing whatever you felt like doing!"

So our sense of appreciation has become skewed. I think *skewed* is the best word to use, because the lack of discipline in our world makes it difficult for us to properly judge or distinguish something, to give it the level of appreciation that it really deserves. We regard things on an emotional level only, not necessarily on a substantive level. We just look at the fact that somebody had the nerve to do it, then we say, "Come on, everybody, put your hands together!" We've done so much of that for everything and everybody that nobody has to do anything of any consequence anymore for us to put our hands together.

Overscheduling Means Your Priorities Need Adjustment

When I was overworking myself, I was guilty of overscheduling and overcommitment. I would often place conflicting engagements and meetings so close to one another that oftentimes I would book two or three things at the same time, on top of each other, stepping into one meeting or event a bit early and leaving for the second one after it had already begun, only to make the third one before everyone left. What did I need to prove? Did I feel the proverbial sand slipping through my hands? I know that I felt that being busy was a badge of honor.

For many years, I and other overachievers I know bragged about how little sleep we needed. A prominent pastor in my city once quipped to me that sleep was a waste of time. He would say to me, "I've learned how to fall into the REM [rapid eye movement, characteristic of deep sleep] sleep in fifteen minutes, so I don't need as much. I have too much on my mind, too many things to do, and I'm too busy to sleep." He thought that sleep was a nuisance, that he only needed four hours a night. Why is that? Why are we so busy? Is it avoidance? Perhaps the busier you are, the less emotionally and physically available you have to be to those whom you don't want to spend much time with.

We can be only so multifaceted and multitasked before something in our lives begins to suffer. Often the first casualty is the closest thing to you: your family. The time, the attention, and the small expressions that make big impressions are lost. You begin missing your children's sports, music, and creative arts events for what seem like legitimate excuses. You begin to regard work and even ancillary engagements as being more important—especially if some level of compensation is involved. Then your professional life, in your estimation, becomes more important than a child's recital or football game, more urgent than a wife's Employee Night. You regularly pass up the quality time that a family expects and deserves. But if you find yourself bragging about the boards and committees on which you serve, don't confuse "busy" with "effective." Benjamin Franklin said that we get old too soon and wise too late.

Each of us has 168 hours per week to use as we see fit. Therefore, each of us must be guided by our own core values and life priorities. You must set boundaries for other people's desires for you and the culmination of their agendas.

Overcome approval addictions and work martyrdom. When faced with the question of accepting or rejecting an addition to your calendar, ask yourself these questions: Does thinking about this activity energize me or drain me? How is this activity serving me or helping me to grow? So before you accept something new on the calendar, fully accept responsibility for it. This exercise will give you a greater appreciation for the power of "no" as well.

I can't live people's lives for them, nor can I fill in all of their gaps.

I must learn as others do how to delegate that which is less significant and remain focused on that which is essential and important.

My own overwhelming, overscheduled calendar was my fault. I did it to myself.

YOUR CHILDREN NEED A BREAK TOO

One of the big things now is getting control of the children's schedule. Nowadays, even our kids are overscheduled. They're in dance, they're in ballet, they're on the soccer team. They have daily practice, then they have games and concerts and recitals to attend. When we were kids, we went outside and played—and that was it. We invented games. We would play with jacks, marbles, and yo-yos, and we jumped rope. We became creative. We could find a stick and an old raggedy ball in the alley and play a game of stickball. We just learned how to do stuff and just play. When those streetlights came on, that was it. Playtime was over, and we went home. There was really no pressure to perform or to compete. Yes, we chose sides and played ball on separate teams, but there was more emphasis on teamwork.

Now it's more individualistic, more about individual performance. Parents are pushing their kids into different areas, priming them for scholarships. That becomes the motivation now: I've got you on the basketball team, because I think you can get a basketball scholarship. When my daughter was on her high school swimming team, the best swimmer on the team was a young lady whose father drove her like Sergeant Carter in the old *Gomer Pyle* TV sitcom. He would yell at her from the sidelines, even to the point of cussing her out! He was taking it way too seriously. I soon realized that he was trying to steer her toward a college scholarship so that he wouldn't have to pay the tuition!

This more serious approach from parents toward their children's activities is the reason for most of the overscheduling young people are experiencing. Parental expectations are over the top. We used to just let the kids get involved for physical fitness and for the benefits of competition. But now, we're determined to make them professionals from the day they are born.

SPINNING PLATES AT THE CIRCUS

I once went to a circus and observed a tremendously talented performer spinning plates on poles without allowing them to fall off or even to slow down much. As the plates were spun, they had a gyroscopic effect. The skill that the performer exhibited was that he was able to maintain equilibrium and velocity while he did the same spin on the other poles and plates. The performer was also a gifted contortionist. He spun the plates, added new poles, and added plates, all while displaying incredible physical agility, balance, and coordination. He then incorporated acrobatic moves, as he balanced the poles and kept the plates spinning, seeking never to let a plate fall and break. The more plates he would spin, the more frantic and stressful it became for him to dash from one plate to another plate to keep them all spinning. If any one of the plates slowed down too much, it would fall and break. The seemingly impossible task was for the performer to constantly evaluate which plates were spinning well and which plates were trending toward disaster. He had to continue to make split-second decisions on how best to keep all the plates and all the poles functioning.

Being reminded of that circus performer, I saw a symbiotic thread between that entertaining act under the big tent and my own reality. My imagination replaces the performer with me. I imagine that the plates are work, physical health, family, business pursuits, etc. Often we are like circus performers, running frantically between responsibilities and commitments, trying to keep every plate spinning that we've taken on. A little spin here and a little spin there; don't let any of the plates stop spinning! Lowered velocity will cause them to fall off the poles. Focus on one plate too long and the others will crash to the floor. Try to keep them all spinning at the same velocity and you will collapse out of exhaustion. It can never be sustained over time. Allow the poles and the plates to force you into acrobatic contortions, and you virtually assure breakage at some point.

Overachievers often justify taking on an impossible set of responsibilities that are just as demanding as spinning plates on poles. They do it to prove to others how much agility they have, which is the same motivation that the circus performer has. But notice that just as no one in the audience ever comes up to help the circus performer spin his plates, rarely does anyone step forward to help the overachiever. He has to handle that on his own. That's another irony about people who are overachievers. They never seem to get the help that others get—although they need it the most. People see the overachiever or the workaholic as not needing any help. They see him as having capacity that exceeds theirs. Others sit down and allow overachievers to do everything because they know overachievers can't stand to see gaps that go unfilled.

Multitasking Reconsidered

Psychologists from the American Psychological Association conducted an extensive study on multitasking and learned what happens to cognitive mental processes when people try to perform more than one task at a time. Recent research seems to suggest that the mind and the brain were not designed for heavy-duty multitasking. Research conducted at Stanford University found that multitasking is less productive than doing a single thing at a time. According to the Stanford research, those who multitask a lot and believe that it boosts their performance were actually less productive than those who like to do a single thing at a time. The frequent multitaskers performed worse because they had more trouble organizing their thoughts and filtering out irrelevant information. The Stanford research found that multitasking reduces efficiency and performance, because the brain can only focus on one thing at a time.

When you try to do two major things at once, your brain lacks the capacity to perform both tasks successfully and effectively, according to Dr. Travis Bradbury, author of *Emotional Intelligence 2.0*. The University of Sussex in Brighton, England, compared the amount of time people spend on multiple devices, such as texting on a smartphone while watching TV, to MRI scans of their brains. They found that high multitaskers had less brain density in the anterior singular cortex, a region of the brain responsible for empathy as well as cognitive and emotional control.

The conclusion that I draw from all of this is that more is not more. More is less and less is more. The bandwidth of our brains does not necessarily accommodate multitasking for optimal performance and productivity. So to be at our best, we must learn to focus.

I throw this new and interesting research against the backdrop of the "do more and be better" messages that we've gotten from so many motivational "achievement" books. We have read and heard about "7 Steps to Success," or "10 Steps to Becoming a Great Person," and it always comes down to "you've got to do more" and "you need to add this to your list." If you want to be a successful business owner or a dynamic entrepreneur, if you want to be whatever it is that fulfills your dreams and live your best life now, you've got to do more, more, more, more! Not only is that message unrealistic, but also we now find that recent studies suggest that the more we put on our brains, the more we fill brain capacity that is quite limited—until we take intentional steps to expand it.

A good analogy would be comparing our brain capacity with a phone or a computer that only has a certain amount of gigabytes. We understand that those electronic products have a certain capacity for information and no more. Normally, when you even approach the threshold of that capacity, you start having problems with your device. A computer gets really slow, for instance. That device begins to try to tell you, "I am reaching capacity—and I can only do so much. In order for me to work optimally I have to have additional capacity, freed-up capacity. There are things that have to be deleted in order for me to be productive and effective." So even the digital machine you depend upon each day will start acting crazy, start malfunctioning, start slowing down.

How many of us reach our thresholds and begin to slow down the rate and the cadence of our productivity, becoming less and less effective? How many great minds have been dulled by excess work, excess information, lack of focus, and heavy multitasking? How much of this has sapped the strength of gifted, talented, imaginative people?

The mistake that people make is trying to expanding their portfolios before they expand capacity. When that happens, the result usually amounts to trouble. What everyone should remember is not to expand a portfolio until you've expanded capacity. Otherwise, you're headed for a breakdown or a loss of productivity. Or your core systems will begin to slow in such a way that you become totally ineffective.

Psychologists tell us that we really only use about 10 percent of our brains. Maybe even some of the smartest people among us are perhaps at 15 percent. So the thing is, until we develop and increase our brain capacity, there's only so much we can take on anyway. We could do a lot more if our brains were developed to do so. But until we go out of our way to stretch and expand our brainpower, we will always default to the 10 percent level, because capacity has to be developed first.

Building capacity is like lifting weights on a regular basis in order to prepare for a demanding contact sport or a weight-lifting competition. What would I look like trying to bench-press three hundred pounds when I don't have the muscular capacity or the experience to do that? Why would I take that on when that's an inordinate amount of pressure that I'm putting on myself that is totally unnecessary and not sustainable? I mean, I'd kill myself or suffer a bad injury trying to do it.

We can apply the lesson of being focused to organizations as well. Most businesses that have been highly successful for long periods of time started with a simple thing. 3M began as Minnesota Mining and Manufacturing—before striking it rich with transparent, easy-to-use Scotch tape. But, of course, they increased their capacity over time and expanded their portfolio to include many other products. A corporation making a certain thing might say, "We do a good job making that product. Now we're branching off and doing something new. And we're going to get bigger by buying another company." But they can't do all of that until they focus and establish initial success where they are.

The challenge of establishing focus can be compared to playing a bingo card. I figure the more bingo cards I have in front of me, the greater chance I have of winning. If I get one bingo card, it's a slow drag. But if I get ten bingo cards in front of me, and you say B57, I know it's probably on one of those cards! So I'm excited. Yet it's never that easy. When the dealer calls the number, all of a sudden I'm searching and fumbling around, trying to figure out which card it's on. My big plan kind of turns into the spinning plates syndrome. Many of us do that all of time—setting before ourselves all of these bingo cards, trying to manage all of these different things at one time. As I recall from playing bingo years ago, when the number is called, you're only given a certain amount of time in order to place your chip on the card before the caller moves on to the next number. And so the thing is, you've got ten bingo cards and you're trying to look for B57 and you say, "Wait a minute. Hold it! Hold up! I think I've got B57 here somewhere!"

Too many people do just that in their quest for success. They put before themselves too many bingo cards, often thinking that they need to keep a lot in motion, in order to have something to "fall back on.' They let the multiple bingo cards slow them down. They are constantly busy, but their productivity and mental sharpness suffer, just like the whole spinning plates thing. If I can spin a plate with this finger, then what about that finger? What about through my legs? What about behind my head and behind my back? What if I contort myself and do it, trying to really impress the crowd? We see people like on *America's Got Talent* or some of these shows where they're looking to find people with unusual talent. But, of course, everybody is not gifted to spin plates. Or to play bingo! Not with that many cards. So the reality is that with excessive multitasking, often we're really working against ourselves.

If you're going to be "spinning plates on poles" in your personal life, you may as well make it manageable for yourself by making focus a priority.

CHAPTER 5

FOCUS: MAINTAINED BY DISCIPLINE

What Is Focus?

Focus is about choosing a few things at a time and doing them well. Focus is about the following things:

- envisioning an expectation;
- aiming for a specific purpose;
- execution, arriving at a measurable goal or outcome;
- achieving a desired result.

Focus is the fruition of a determined plan. It is not a set of bingo cards, nor a plethora of poles and spinning plates.

Focus illuminates the center, the focal point, of interest or activity. Focus unveils a clear definition and often makes plain a clear destination. It is a thinking and organizing skill that prioritizes tasks and directs attention and effort. Focus is a strategy that eliminates distraction and channels input. It is a concept of management and governance. Focus is aim, intent. Life must become intentional and focused to be managed well. Focus allows us to maximize efficiencies and ensure desired outcomes.

THE IMPORTANCE OF DISCIPLINE

Discipline is a big part of the process of prioritizing—where I begin to understand which is *most* important and what is *least* important, based upon a system of hierarchy. Discipline helps us to be able to fully analyze things and place them in perspective. Discipline helps us to form a system of belief in our lives that lets us differentiate things, so that we know what is important and what is not. Discipline provides a consistent way of operating, a consistent way of doing things, that helps me to understand the value of things. Discipline makes us much more productive.

One key to my journey is the fact that I was raised in a very strict family where discipline was high on the list of expectations. There were many rules and many regulations in my household, to which we children were expected to adhere directly. Sometimes a disciplinary atmosphere and environment causes people to believe that they're not given an opportunity to be themselves, or that they're not given an opportunity to express themselves. But I never took it that way. I grew to recognize that discipline helps me to be my highest self.

Even when I was younger, I noticed that other families, in my estimation, didn't have discipline. I noticed how dysfunctional they seemed to be. I can't say that I always loved my family's rules and regulations, because what kid wants discipline? But I came to appreciate what discipline means, and what it does in the life of an individual. And I began to see the fruits of discipline. I think that sometimes people don't see the fruit of it until they notice someone who has consistently applied it to his or her own life.

One of my attributes, I believe, is consistency. I think that if people were playing a game and they were supposed to use one word to describe me, that word would be *consistent*. My consistency is directly attributable to the discipline that I had as a child. It's what I was always expected to do. For me, being exceptional was normal. Exceptional was expected. So, when I did something exceptional, it was regarded as something that I was supposed to do.

Owning It: Personal Responsibility and Accountability

Discipline is best incorporated into a person's lifestyle when that person lives up to his or her requirements by first *owning up* to the fact that those requirements exist. All of us have a level of personal responsibility and accountability that, if neglected, brings serious consequences. That simple fact is a missing narrative in our culture these days. We rarely hear the statement made in an honest, fair, nonthreatening way: "You're responsible."

Responsibility has its rewards; irresponsibility has its ramifications. Personal responsibility, by definition, is the idea that human beings choose, instigate, or otherwise cause their own realities. So there has to be a clear commitment to personal accountability. We start as babies in the world, accountable to no one, with no personal responsibility whatsoever. Everything is done for us. When we are children, we learn how to tie our shoes, how to make up a bed, how to keep our clothes off the floor. We're taught to go to school and to be attentive and successful there. Each task becomes our responsibility. Proving that we will consistently do what we've been taught becomes an accountability. We quickly learn that responsibility has rewards and that irresponsibility in anything or any area of our lives has ramifications and penalties. But too often, we learn that the hard way.

If I'm a diabetic, I know that I shouldn't eat a gallon of ice cream, because I know that works against me. If I have high blood pressure, I know that I've got to lower it and keep it controlled through a combination of medication, losing weight, eating well, cutting down on sodium, and doing a bunch of other things. If I'm irresponsible with the salt shaker and I eat a slab of ribs every night, then I know that I'm working against myself; I'm literally engaging in self-sabotage, and my level of irresponsibility is going to have penalties.

* * * * * * *

A financial advisor listens to your goals, your life plan, and then develops a financial strategy for you to follow to achieve those goals. In order to ultimately attain those financial outcomes and to finance, let's say, your retirement, you'll have to pay a monthly calculated amount that is designated in the advisor's plan. To deviate from or not to execute the plan is to fail—because the metrics and the calculations are based on real numbers, and numbers don't lie. So the venom that you render against the advisor for not achieving the goal is useless and baseless, because you have to own the failure yourself.

The dentist always encourages patients to floss as well as to brush. Brushing is essential for regular oral hygiene, but flossing is the ultimate. It loosens and takes out plaque, bacteria, and other nefarious particles that brushing will not. So the dentist strongly urges you to floss because the accumulated, unaddressed plaque and other particles over time could ruin your teeth and your gums and bring a shorter life span to retaining them. The dentist will give you plenty of floss for free when you visit. But many people have rolls and rolls of floss stockpiled somewhere in the bathroom, because they have not executed the flossing technique. But to berate the dentist for the problems that flossing could have prevented makes no sense. You must own those problems.

A third illustration I'll share is when a doctor prescribes medication to control runaway blood pressure and hypertension. A diagnosis is obtained, and then the patient is told that he or she must lose weight, reduce stress, etc. An approach to attack high blood pressure and successfully manage it is prescribed and a warning is given: uncontrolled blood pressure and unmanaged hypertension causes kidneys to be affected, threatening kidney failure, and increases the preponderance of the onset of diabetes. But consternation directed toward the doctor about deteriorating or debilitating chronic illness is ill-advised and unwarranted. You've been warned! So you must own it.

The rise and fall of a full cast of sports figures and entertainers whose lives have veered off the track of sanity and into incredulity is often mind-boggling. Much can be said about the pressures to perform, the intoxication of fame, and the lifestyles that ambulate in dimensions that are uncommon and unfamiliar to the average person. Megawealth is an added factor that can pervert and undermine the strongest ethical and cognitive mind. Often, the important life decisions and tricky ethical questions that must be decided are left for a star's handlers and "posse" members to make, as the star is encouraged to home in on the craft that brings in the revenue that allows the handlers and close associates to exist. Yet the Hall of Famer, the marquee entertainer, and the rap mogul all have to own it. Otherwise, what seems to be a privileged life becomes a journey to the bottom.

Personal responsibility and accountability is absolutely essential. You've got to own that for yourself in order to be successful. The bottom line is that you're totally responsible for your life. This principle, this reality, this foundational premise is essential to life itself and for any attempt at successful work-life integration. Blaming others is not an option. Excuses fuel failure. Quit playing the blame game. Own it!

Passion and Purpose Fulfillment

I want to encourage you to begin making decisions that help you to become more productive and more effective, in order to reach a level where your life has greater meaning and greater purpose. How do I fulfill my purpose if I'm always fulfilling somebody else's purpose for them? If everybody else is determining my purpose, what my priorities are, and how my time is going to be spent, then naturally they will want my priorities to be theirs. In their eyes, the most meaningful thing that I can do will be what *they* say—not that I fulfill my own purpose.

It's important for me, number one, to know my own purpose. Number two, it's important for me to set forth a system that determines how I arrive at that purpose. Number three, I need to put some passion toward the purpose; I've got to put myself into it. But I can't put myself into the passion and the purpose for which I was created and for which I am intended—the intent that God had when He created me—if, in fact, I am fulfilling everyone else's dreams. Therefore, if we are to fulfill the dreams that God has placed inside of us, there must be a discipline, a prioritization, and a balance that has to be attached to those dreams. This is one of the most important points that you can take from *I Did It to Myself.*

Think about it: whenever I say yes to someone else, I'm saying yes to what their agenda is. Please don't take me wrong. I'm not being selfish or haughty or anything like that. I'm just saying that, having come so close to an abrupt end to my life, I now realize how much time and energy I had been spending on the fulfillment of other people's agendas. Not that my involvement wasn't honorable or noble. And I tried to avoid attaching myself to anything frivolous. But recently I have thoughtfully considered how many people I advised, counseled, put in the spotlight, and supported financially, in ways that strategically helped them to reach their goals. I am not saying that there shouldn't be mutuality in a friendship, in a community, in a church. I'm going to support people, and I hope that people will support me. I get that. But when there's an imbalance and I'm always giving much more than I get, then, pretty soon, I'll be losing who I am.

I think that's pretty succinct: if you find yourself losing who you are, ultimately you will lose your passion. That's because your passion is tied to your destiny. More specifically, the passion that you have is tied to whatever your purpose is. So God gives me a passion to match my purpose. My purpose is fueled by my passion. But if I'm expending all of my passion in somebody else's purpose, then I lose my own sense of purpose and direction, my identity, and my own forward mobility. Passion has to be managed. It should not be bridled, but it does have to be managed.

DISCIPLINE IN THE "OFF-SEASON"

What do you do when you're gifted and talented and you're in the off-season? That is, you've been training and preparing for a specific task, but the opportunity to actually do it has not yet arrived? Your discipline will have to drive you then. How you schedule yourself, how you plan your life, will make the difference.

Some people just sit back and allow life to come at them. Other people tell themselves, *I'm going to go out and meet the challenge or opportunity before it arrives.* It's the same principle that you see in play when you go to the airport. At the luggage carousel in baggage claim, when you see your bag, you begin to position yourself to retrieve it. You don't just stand there and let the thing come all the way around. No, no, no, no! You begin to brace yourself, and then you position yourself to grab your luggage when it comes around. You can't help it: you start moving toward the bag! They say bags look alike, and they do. But 90 percent of the time, you can see your bag when it's far away. You know it's yours. It's black just like the rest of them, but you know it's your bag. Whether you've got some distinguishing characteristic on it or not, you know it's yours. But how many people have missed their luggage by not positioning themselves to retrieve it? They have to wait a good while before it comes back around.

Set a schedule; set a timetable. The most optimum way to receive results in your life is to do what you do in a disciplined manner. Even if you're gifted, even if you're spontaneous, and even if you are "uninhibited" or unlimited in terms of your gift, it's best to set some goals and parameters. The artist needs discipline. He or she needs a plan.

So that discipline, that balance, that placing myself on a plan and a schedule is extremely important to reach what I want to call *extenuated* success. You have a lot of flashes in the pan, a lot of shooting stars. But we're talking about longevity. I know something about that, as a person who has persevered. There are not a whole lot of people left who have been at one church for forty years. That just doesn't happen much anymore.

I think that it's very important to have a message to people about these intangibles. The discipline, the balance of life, really matters. I can tell you that my sickness, my physical struggles, taught me some life lessons. One of those lessons is that there comes a point in your life that no matter what you have accomplished, you begin to understand what truly matters. And when you discover what really matters, here's what happens: you find that the list is extremely short. What really matters is a short list. When we're younger, we think that everything is important; everything is a big deal. But what time and the kind of experience that I've been through will show you is that eventually you must be selective about what is a big deal. Now I have to be selective. I have to balance and discipline myself so I'll know what is most important and what is not. I'm in charge of that. I'm in control of what really matters. So it's important that we have the opportunity to sit and prepare ourselves, and prioritize things. That means that I have to learn how to turn some things down.

REDUCING STRESS THROUGH DELEGATION AND ACCOUNTABILITY

We can take important lessons from how large organizations manage growth. When companies grow, they have specific benchmarks, metrics, and strategies to accommodate their successes. They outsource nonrelated business units like HR, transportation, food, security, and IT services. When you as an individual reach similar places of growth and expansion, how do you outsource the stress, the weight of this trajectory of growth? Furthermore, how do you know when to do it? In other words, if a company or large organization knows how to do that, and if I, as an overwhelmed person, am the manager or even the CEO of a high-growth organization, then why am I not using that same concept to manage and balance myself?

The leader of an organization may not necessarily be the most talented person; many times leaders learn how to depend on the people around them better than most. I know a CEO who has technical expertise and knows his industry, but he has excelled mainly because he has surrounded himself with top managers who have people skills that he does not have. That is to his credit. He realizes his deficit—and we all have them—but he's put the right people around him. What separates him from a frustrated, unsuccessful leader is the focus and discipline to delegate.

Making yourself accountable to others is a practice that, like delegation, increases productivity. A creative high achiever, to have maximum impact, often must work closely with a more detailed person who is attuned to the logistical process. I think the more talented you are, the more gifted you are, the more you need somebody who is going to keep you grounded. You need somebody who's going to keep your feet on the ground so that you don't lose sight of who you are and where you are. That's part of the equilibrium we all need: someone in our lives who holds us accountable. Too often, people don't have the right relationships.

There's a Bible story in the book of Acts about a young man who went to church and fell asleep as the apostle Paul was preaching. This young man fell out of the window—a terrible emergency for him and for that church. His mishap teaches us several things that are very important but very simple. One: be careful where you sleep. Church is not a good place to sleep—it's a place that requires your attentiveness. Two: be careful whom you sit beside. Make sure that you find a seatmate who holds you accountable, who will say, "Hey, wake up!" That young man should have been sitting by someone who would make sure that he wouldn't go to sleep. Three: be careful how you sit in church. This young man had one foot in the window and one foot out of the window. (Of course, there's an old proverb about people who've got one foot in the church and one foot out of the church. You've got to be all the way in.)

Now, of course, the beauty of that text is that when the young man fell out of that window, he fell three stories down and died—literally. Yet the Bible says that Paul left the third level, went outside, covered him, and spoke life over him. The young man came back to life. That's kind of my story. I recovered from a sudden death. The church should always have somebody who can speak life into people who fall out of the window—who have one foot in and one foot out, or who somehow get off track.

Whether or not our realm of operation is a community like a church, we all need an accountability source near us—a partner or a staff member or somebody else who will say, "Hey, stay on task" or "Go home! Go get your rest. That's enough for today." Rhonda, my executive assistant, is that kind of person for me. She will say, "You know, that's it. That conference call or that last appointment is your last guy. Go home!"

So when I came back to work after being sick, I had to abbreviate my schedule. I still have to get the stuff done that has to be done, and I've still got to meet with the people I've got to meet with, but Rhonda has been much more strategic in planning my schedule and spreading out my commitments for me so that I don't try to do it all in one day. I don't overwhelm myself now; thanks, Rhonda!

DELEGATION: HOW TO BUILD A $25 MILLION CHURCH

During the construction of my church's current building, a beautiful, $25 million facility, two men with unique backgrounds came to my church and became members. One of them was a project manager for construction at the Detroit Medical Center. The other was a project manager for a private construction company.

I noticed that one of the guys joined the male chorus to sing with the men. I approached him and said, "Hey brother, how you doin'? Just wanted to introduce myself—I'm Pastor Vann," and so on.

"Oh yeah? My name is Chuck Lewis. I'm happy to be here," he answered.

"Well, what do you do?" I asked.

"I'm a project manager for a construction company," he said.

Here was an executive of a construction company whose CEO is a guy I went to school with. And I'm in the middle of building a church!

"The kingdom needs your expertise," I told him. "I don't need you in the choir! As a matter of fact, come with me."

I made him come to my office and I told the choir folks, "Look, he's no longer in the choir. I've got something for him to do."

Chuck, the former choir member, was more than happy to make the switch. Because what he could do for the building project was the kind of work he did every day.

The other fellow who joined the church was a wonderful guy whom I later made one of my trustees. I asked him one day, "Man, what do you do?"

He said, "Oh, I'm a construction manager for the Detroit Medical Center."

I said, "What?"

At the time, Mike Duggan was CEO of the medical center. (In 2013, a few years later, he was elected mayor of Detroit—his current office.) So I went to Mike and made the same request that I'd made to the construction company CEO, who had been my classmate in high school.

I told both of them, "Look here: your guys, I need them! I'm building a church. I need them in my construction meeting every Tuesday with my project manager, the architect, the whole thing. I know all about running a church, but I don't know how to build one." I mean, a $25 million construction project? Nope, I don't know how to do that! And I'm not stupid enough to pretend that I do, like some preachers are.

So I asked both organizations to lend those two guys to me pro bono. If they would pay them, I'd put them to work every Tuesday. Both groups gave me ten hours a week for both of them. So I ended up with twenty hours of professional expertise for nothing! That's the reason that my new church was built on time and on budget. It was the discipline of proper planning, organization, and decision-making that experienced people brought to the table. I recognized the expertise that I needed, that

God had sent me, in order to make this work. The project was not going to get done on time or on budget just because I sat in on a construction meeting every Tuesday. Instead, I was going to waste money, I was going to waste time, and I was going to misuse my own talents by trying to do something I wasn't qualified to do. Construction management is not my gift; it's not my expertise. So I learned the art of delegation.

I learned how to reach for the right people at the right time to fulfill the assignment. That's a skill. That has to become a skill for everyone who wants to do great things. That's a skill set. It is essential if your goal is to bring your life back into balance—as I've had to do—after years of trying to do too much. When you do, you'll be in a position to really put your affairs in order, to actually get more work done, and to work smarter and not harder.

The art of delegation is a strategy for reaching that abundant life that we've been promised. It's important that we understand the power of partnership. We don't need any more churches that are personality driven, where the pastor tries to micromanage everything. That kind of organization is unhealthy for everyone involved.

I now recognize that when I say no, many times I am setting a proper parameter between what I'm gifted to do, purposed to do, and intended to do, and what I do not have as a gift or purpose or talent.

STAYING IN YOUR LANE IS A KINGDOM IMPERATIVE

Unfortunately, what we don't do enough of in the church is steer people toward responsible secular careers, which to me is a kingdom imperative. I will tell you what I told an experienced Christian writer who helped me produce this book. The way I see it, the kingdom needs journalists. The kingdom needs writers and editors like him. He helped me to articulate the important messages that I am sharing with you. During our talks together, I reminded him that his expertise was helping me to package my purpose. That is, by putting my insights and opinions into the proper form, his work has helped me to fulfill my purpose to the world. My hope is that the result will be significant impact, in some form, upon your life and the lives of other readers.

The thing is that God knows, right now, where each of us is supposed to be and what each of us is supposed to do. We are by no means robots, but you might say that each of us is born "programmed" to move forward in a certain direction. Our tendencies come from our parents and our ancestors, as well as from our environment. But God knows what each of us can best offer to the world during our time here. Unless—as a result of some unfortunate misguidance—we begin to do things that don't come naturally to us, we will fulfill our purpose by simply doing what we enjoy, doing what we are good at, taking advantage of opportunities before us.

Yet the church world has too often been a hindrance to the natural development of an individual's divine purpose. As I told the Christian writer I worked with, in some church circles—especially in years past—he would be advised to go into the ministry, rather than excel in the communications field. Too many of us would tell someone like him, "Put that pen down. Put that tape recorder down, son. You've got a call on your life, boy! Don't you know you're supposed to be preaching? We need you right here in this church; there's work for you to do!"

This kind of "career guidance" used to be very common in the black church, particularly when opportunities for African Americans were limited in the mainstream job market. Thankfully, we don't see that in black culture as much as we once did. However, black churches still don't do a good enough job of lifting up the significance of all of our gifts and talents and abilities—especially now that we have a much more educated populace than we had in old-time black culture. In old-time black culture, the center of the community was the church. The church was the source of opportunity, and many people felt they had to leave the church—drop their membership—to get some other kind of an opportunity.

However, I believe that we ought to have a kingdom mind-set. The kingdom mind-set sees the gifts and talents all of us have as essential to glorifying God on earth, not merely as tools that we put to work in the secular workplace.

You might be familiar with a teaching known as Seven Mountains. It is a concept developed in 1975 by Bill Bright, founder of Campus Crusade for Christ, and Loren Cunningham, founder of Youth with a Mission. Bright and Cunningham identified "seven mountains of societal influence" that exist in every nation: religion, family, education, government, media, arts and entertainment, and business. Their belief is that Christians needed to seek significant influence in—indeed, dominance over—each of these areas if the kingdom of God is to be established in the nation.*

I recently met with a lady who leads one of America's top regional charitable foundations. She is a young black woman who graduated from a top law school, worked for a well-known nonprofit organization, and also worked at the highest levels of federal government. During our get-acquainted meeting I learned that she is a well-grounded Christian, as well. I was so impressed with her that I teasingly told her, "Young lady, you don't know how significant you really are!"

My point is this: we *need* kingdom citizens like her over that important foundation and at the head of many more charitable foundations—because those institutions are the source of valuable resources. The work of the kingdom has to be financed. *How* is it going to get financed? Well, it won't be financed solely by the offerings that people give on Sunday morning! It's going to get financed by bigger sources of wealth. The Bible says that kingdom wealth is transferred from earthly sources. So the thing is, we have to be in the positions of authority where that wealth exists! I think that God has to place us there according to our abilities and skills. We've built generations of church folks who are faithful members and are good at praising the Lord. They sing, clap, and shout in our services, but too often that's all that they know. Unfortunately, too many church members don't know how to live! Their lives are empty.

I love the church and church culture. I was born in the church and I will die in the church. But there's much more to me than just church. I'm not a "preacher period." I'm a "preacher *comma!*" I don't see the world through only one lens. I have a brain, I can think, and I know something about a lot of different arenas of life. I'm familiar with more than theology, the Bible, and how to put together a good sermon and deliver it in the pulpit. I know the intricacies of city, state, and federal government. I know the intricacies of business. So I have other gifts to be used in other ways that are still for the benefit and the aggrandizement of the kingdom. We, as kingdom keepers, ought to be encouraging people who have gifts and expertise to use them not only for their livelihood but also for the kingdom of God! We should teach them that they have something to give back—and it is not necessarily being an usher at the door.

CHAPTER 6
PERSONAL STRATEGIES FOR BEATING STRESS

BALANCE IN AN AMBITIOUS SCHEDULE

Balance makes life manageable. It does not eliminate or obfuscate the pursuit of goals, dreams, aspirations, or ambitions. But balance does obliterate the clutter of busyness and the overwhelming sense of obligation. The clutter is like a closet with a plethora of empty hangers. The opportunity is there for a more structured, user-friendly closet environment, but the clutter of questionable hangers muddies the process. Clutter often puts the management of goals beyond reach, so that they don't ever manifest.

Balance is not multitasking. Balance presupposes that there is a threshold as to how much can be taken on, based on one's capacity and ability to perform and properly execute.

Consider the stanchions that regulate crowd control and human traffic at an airport security checkpoint. Those series of posts, connected by ropes or bands, balance the traffic to keep it manageable. Eventually, everybody gets through, but the stanchions set parameters and establish the process for *how* they get through. The balance they create makes the airport manageable.

In order to balance, a tightrope walker must shift her weight constantly to maintain equilibrium and steadiness. Balance is correct and proper proportionality. Life doesn't stop at work and work doesn't stop at home for successful people. Success is often an amalgamation of it all. It is a tapestry, not a separate fabric.

"So many people spend their health gaining wealth, and then have to spend their wealth to regain their health."* So said A. J. Reb Materi, a Canadian administrator in the Roman Catholic diocese of Saskatoon, Saskatchewan, in what has become a world-famous quote by a less-than-famous individual. Balance comes when you aspire to and pursue the life of your passion, by making the choices that align with the life that you seek. You may have heard the adage "When you are born, you look like your parents. When you die, you look like your decisions."

Extremes are easy, but balance is often much more tedious. Balance must be something that you create. I've heard that during his eight years in office, President Barack Obama's schedule normally consisted of only four to six things a day. His desk was never cluttered. He only dealt with the things that he *had* to deal with. His early morning cabinet meeting began with the president's security briefing, a highly classified document prepared by the national security director. Obama probably got a briefing from a key cabinet officer about an issue that was current. He might have gotten a briefing from the White House staff or congressional leaders on his legislative strategy. He might have delivered remarks to some select group of citizens. And he might have had to focus on a particular unscheduled issue for that day. But that was a typical day, and every day has unique challenges for the person in the toughest job in the world.*

Compare that with what used to be my typically overloaded schedule. I had ten meetings a day scheduled on my calendar, almost every day. I was also doing administrative duties *and* staff meetings *and* special events *and* projects *and* capital campaigns, also building a multimillion-dollar facility in a recession, finding time for dinner with my wife every day, and dealing with my kids, talking to them and being a good dad—even after they were grown. I was working day and night, twelve to fourteen hours a day, until my body began to send signals. Like text messages, you see on the log who's sending them, but you don't want to open the messages, because you just about know the nature of the content. It was at that point that I was made to lie down.

Many times people who position themselves as "work martyrs" are people who are encouraged to continue to do things the way they've been doing them. They get recognition for it. People say, "Wow, he's such a good guy. Man, he sure does a lot. He takes care of it all, doesn't he?"

Eventually the workaholic's staff members will tell each other, "Don't you worry about that; he'll take care of that." But that kind of imbalanced leadership ends up being an insult to others, because it encroaches on the other team members' spheres of responsibility. By contrast, when the leader's work-life integration is on target, the rest of the team has a balanced sense of responsibility on the job. No one has to burn out.

WORK-LIFE INTEGRATION

I've been using that phrase *work-life integration* off and on throughout this book. Let me better explain what it means to me. Perfect balance in every area of life is the ideal that each of us is shooting for. But life comes at you imbalanced, haphazardly, and often without warning. Most societies now look at life not in the traditional sense of "balance," but in the contemporary sense of work-life integration. Balance is the even distribution of weight, enabling someone or something to remain upright, steady, and stable. Balance infers the traditional image of a scale with equalized weight. It can be thought of as one world competing against the other, with a vertical axis in the middle. But what most of us desire today is work-life integration: achieving a workable relationship between the many competing commitments in our lives, one that allows us to follow a vocation that fulfills a calling and also participate in personal activities and relationships that bring us happiness and fulfillment.

To integrate is to form, coordinate, or blend into a functioning or unified whole. The modern ideal is to have our professional and personal lives organically blended. That's the new reality. Life in this technological age cannot be lived in compartmentalized silos. Life in the twenty-first century is a dynamic, ever evolving, often exciting, never mundane, always-in-motion flow of instant connectivity, instant demands, instant information, instant access, and instant gratification. Boundaries, limitations, and parameters are now blurred and synthesized. Work life and personal life, and work and leisure, now intersect. Work-life balance is not the sum of two equal parts. It is a roving, daily recalculation.

Josh Linkner's Three Lists

Josh Linkner, a prominent high-tech entrepreneur, venture capitalist, and author, has written that "the 24-hour clock is a brutal, unforgiving foe."* I'm intrigued by Linkner's suggestion that to make better use of the limited time available to us, everyone should draw up three lists.*

- Number one is the *more* list. Ask yourself: What do I need to do more of? What, in your opinion, has the highest value? Make a list of the top seven things you want to prioritize and concentrate on.

- Number two should be the *less* list. What do you need less of? What seven items or activities should be reduced or eliminated from your life?

- Number three is the *stop* list. This list should contain the things you do that you should stop doing. This list should include the least valuable things that you do, time wasters that you should eliminate—and people with whom you should stop interacting.

The Power of No

I did not learn until my near-death experience how to turn things down. I didn't say no to people; I never learned how to say, "I'm not going to have time to do that." I never learned how to tell my assistant, "No, I'm not available for that." *Well, do you have anything else on your calendar?* "No. That's time I need to prepare. I have an important meeting coming up, and I need to think through some key issues," etc. If I add something else to my calendar, then I won't have time to prepare.

Billionaire investor Warren Buffett has said that successful people say yes very often, in order to make themselves available to the optimum number of opportunities. Yet those folks don't last in the long run, Buffett said. The difference between successful people and *really* successful people is that really successful people say no to just about everything, he said.* That means that they're much more prescriptive about what they take on. I think that truth is quite profound when we take a broad view of business enterprise.

Once, I had a chance to be in the room when Oprah Winfrey was telling a group a story about the power of saying no. She said, "One day I got a call from Stevie Wonder," the Grammy-winning music legend. Her first thought was about her excitement: *Stevie Wonder? Whew!* She said Stevie wanted her to be part of a business proposal he had developed. She told his representative to send all of the relevant materials to her office so that her staff could engage in a due diligence examination. Her staff eventually advised her not to get involved. But Stevie kept calling, Oprah said.

She wondered, "How do you tell Stevie Wonder no?" So she reached out to poet and friend Maya Angelou for the answer. Maya Angelou told her that she just had to get comfortable with the answer no, and stick to it. Oprah recalled her saying, "You're not required to get on every bandwagon that comes your way. You're not required to get on every bus. It's not your bus!" I thought it was interesting that an entertainment icon like Oprah admitted. "Even I get offered stuff that I find it hard to say no to."

WRITE DOWN YOUR THOUGHTS

Write, write, write! Write down your thoughts. Write down your schedule. Journaling is key. It can help you analyze how you spend your time.

When I used to have a Franklin planner and write every day in it, I saw how much activity I was engaged in. It helped me to understand the gravity of my choices. A schedule that is digitized on the computer is helpful and efficient, but I still think that handwriting has some residual benefit in terms of permitting us to recognize what we're doing and how much we're doing. It puts your personal energy and endorsement into it. There's something about writing it down yourself that is a little bit more weighty than seeing it on the screen. Seeing it on the screen makes an activity look less tedious and less complicated than it may be. There's something about writing that reveals the true magnitude of your commitment. It helps you to get control of your schedule.

Take Control of Your Calendar

My calendar is a battle zone. It's a nonstop moving target. It's an elusive object for me. But you *must* take control of your calendar. At one point, my calendar became almost a nightmare for my executive staff. I guess I was raised to believe that you don't tell people no. You are always ready and available to do what you can to help people. So I got in the habit of saying to myself, "Wow, this could be a great opportunity!"

As a result, everyone else had control of what mattered to me. I have to admit that I was a slave to the seduction of other people's schedules. Everyone else was determining my passions, priorities, and objectives. How do I know that? Because your schedule determines what matters. It determines your values. What do I value most? It's what I spend my time doing. It's what I spend my money on.

But now my calendar works for me, not against me. I've discovered two important steps that will help you control your calendar, rather than let your calendar to control you.

1. Establish priorities. Even opportunities must be prioritized. Do they fit into your adopted life plan? Are the priorities based upon your values? Make a list of those motivating values. Is it career growth? Is it money? Is it family? Then compare it with what's on your schedule: activities and events, board meetings, etc. When commitments of time and resources don't match your values, ask yourself: does this meeting, activity, or event move me closer to my stated and adopted goals? If it doesn't, then say no without any trepidation.

2. Never confirm a yes immediately. Slow the process down first before scheduling the event. Resist the urge to people-please. What I do now is defer to Rhonda, my executive assistant. She has become a stopgap for everything.

    When somebody comes to me and says, "We'd love for you to preach for us," I say, "I'd love to! When is it?"

    "Oh, it's February 4."

"Really? All right. Well, that sounds good to me. Tell you what: If I'm available, I'll be there. You need to call my office, though, and speak with Rhonda."

Later, after checking my schedule, I might go back and say to Rhonda, "Look, I don't want to do that. I've got too much going on that particular weekend. That's not something I want to do. Tell them no."

I've learned that it's best not to give people a confirmed yes immediately, so that you don't allow people to drag you into decision-making without considering whether the request fits in with your goals, your stated plans, your priorities, or just your time schedule. That's one of the ways I've found that I can conquer this thing.

CHAPTER 7
WHAT LOW-STRESS WORK-LIFE INTEGRATION LOOKS LIKE

Making "Perfect" Health a Reality

I have a pastor friend in Houston, Texas, named Dr. Joe Samuel Ratliff. Dr. Ratliff told an audience the story of a visit to his doctor. After the physician had looked over the results from normal health gauges that measure blood pressure and other vital signs, he told Dr. Ratliff, "You're in good health, but you're in bad shape!" In other words, there were no urgent vital signs to be immediately concerned about, but the pastor's physical fitness left a lot to be desired. His doctor wanted him to lose weight, increase his cardiovascular exercise, and eat smarter. Dr. Ratliff had not reached the point of optimal conditioning that he had the potential to achieve, in his physician's estimation.

At times, we think that perfect health means being Hulk Hogan or some superfit person who runs ten miles every morning or who stays in the gym five hours a day. That's really not what health is. Herophilus, the ancient Greek physician who is often called the father of anatomy, wrote, "When health is absent, wisdom cannot reveal itself, art cannot manifest, strength cannot fight, wealth becomes useless and intelligence cannot be applied." The World Health Organization, an agency of the United Nations, has described health as the state of complete physical, mental, and social well-being, not just merely the absence of disease or infirmity.

Without your health, your passport to life is revoked. Health is the most prized possession one can obtain in life. Yet health is elusive to so many, and it's very hard to regain once a physical crisis manifests in a person's body. Whatever you waste now, you will want later.

So much in our lives is crisis-driven and crisis-manifested, not preventative. Self-care is often neglected, as preparations for other priorities take precedence. But the simple reality is that everything becomes untenable without health. We are not effective if there is something missing and something broken in terms of our health.

Health emanates from the root word *heal*. Of course, the Bible is resplendent with miracles of restored health. Yet maintaining our health is, at a certain level, a matter of spiritual accountability. There is stewardship involved, which means we are responsible for keeping ourselves as healthy as possible. The strength we have when our bodies are well-conditioned is a precious gift.

Therefore, overscheduling, a breakneck pace, lack of exercise, and lack of rest can become a matter of poor stewardship. Bad eating habits and no vacations are the kinds of habits that will ultimately lead to health issues, because you're not in shape. A person's poor physical condition can become a warning—and finally, a wake-up call to change immediately or be shut down involuntarily.

THE HEALTH BENEFITS OF STRESS REDUCTION

Anyone can take a number of positive steps to beat stress and improve health that involve a good diet, regular exercise, and adequate rest. Dr. Eliaz, the holistic physician mentioned earlier, recommends meditation, moderate exercise (such as walking, yoga, and swimming), and proper nutrition as essential. He advocates eating dark greens and foods that provide B-vitamins, magnesium, and calcium, but suggests that caffeine and sugar be avoided, calling them "stimulants" that can "contribute to stress and depression."* He also points to proper sleep and positive thinking as excellent antidotes for stress and its negative effects.

A mental health blog identified ten benefits that come when people reduce stress. Among the benefits identified were the following:

- Cancer prevention, because the immune system is freed to do its job better when stress levels are reduced.*

- A healthier heart: A University of Florida study of patients with heart disease found that they were "less likely to experience a decrease in blood flow to the heart, which can increase the risk of dying three-fold."*

- Lower blood pressure: A sixteen-hour stress-reduction program conducted by the HeartMath Institute of Boulder, Colorado, produced a significant lowering of blood pressure of workers with hypertension, accompanied by greater peace and more hopeful attitudes.*

Other stress-reduction benefits described in the blog article include weight loss, improved sleep, lower levels of aches and pains, increased memory, better relationships, general happiness, and more enthusiasm about life.*

TREATING OURSELVES WELL IS A PREREQUISITE FOR SERVING OTHERS

People who matriculate in people-intensive professions must learn to decompress and de-escalate. Decompression is critical to wholeness and clarity. There should always be a time when you can unplug without feeling guilty. Life is too short to let small things take up so much space. The world will be won by those who are adaptable, having the ability to pivot, to adjust, and to be flexible. Often, there is a price tag to being smart, gifted, or talented. It can make you oblivious to boundaries, capacity, and even pain. Even the extraordinary have a finite capacity. Sometimes, because extraordinary people know that their capacity exceeds that of so many others, it gives them an aura of invincibility. Just about everything will survive if we rest. But the syndrome of "if I don't, it won't" haunts too many of us.

Yet self-care is paramount when you are in the business of serving people. Take inventory of the many ways in which you overextend yourself that lead to stress, ambiguity of purpose, bad health, fuzzy thinking, lack of calmness, and poor eating choices and habits. Balance your life. Can you rest without guilt? For most of my career, I couldn't. I was wound up. And I only seemed to get tighter and tighter. I am wired as a giver, someone who works and serves hard. But I never took the time to replenish that which I have the natural affinity to give.

How do you de-escalate? How do you decompress? The truth is that just about everything will survive if we rest. But the syndrome of "if I don't, it won't" will haunt you if you let it.

Block out "me time" in your schedule. Specify a personal errand, chore, or pleasure you wish to indulge in. Let blocked-out time be used to ingratiate you personally. If I say, "I need to clean the closet," then interrupt that plan by saying, "No, I need to meet with so-and-so," I will never get the closet cleaned because I'm always meeting with someone like so-and-so. Learning how to block out time is one way to attack the overscheduling problem. The key is staying *true* to blocked-out time.

WHAT SCRIPTURE SAYS ABOUT BRINGING ORDER TO A HECTIC LIFE

As a pastor, I naturally believe that proper work-life integration can be best achieved by paying attention to spiritual principles established in God's Word, the Bible.

And the Bible has plenty to say about a well-ordered life where stress is virtually eliminated—even in the toughest of times. Hebrews 12:1 instructs us to lay aside every weight that does so easily beset us and to run with patience—with forethought, with balance, with wisdom—the race that is set before us. Much of the time, all of this busyness is a weight that we're carrying. It's a weight we are dragging with us, almost like a ball and chain. That's where we are when we haven't taken the time to replenish and refresh ourselves. Dropping the weight of constant activity helps us achieve the state of equilibrium that we all want and need to achieve.

Creating order by making rest part of a consistent schedule is a biblical principle established early in the book of Genesis. As explained by the Christian education website GotQuestions.org, God rested on the seventh day of creation (Genesis 2:2–3) as an example for humankind to follow, then made resting on the Sabbath day part of the Hebrew law set forth by Moses (Exodus 20:8–11).* "God desires rest for us because it does not come naturally to us," the website writers note. "To rest, we have to trust that God will take care of things for us. We have to trust that, if we take a day off, the world will not stop turning on its axis."*

Returning to the book of Hebrews, we see that complete faith in Jesus is the ultimate place of rest for believers—in the profound teaching that is set forth from Hebrews 3:7 to Hebrews 4:11. Those who wandered in the desert forty years in the Old Testament are described as disobedient followers who were determined to do things in their own strength, when obedience to God and faith in His instructions would have given them a position of rest. Yet, as New Testament Christians, "we who have believed enter that rest" (Hebrews 4:3). The passage ends with the following exhortation (Hebrews 4:9–11) that equates faith with rest—trusting God's ability rather than our own:

> So then, there remains a Sabbath rest for the people of God, for whoever has entered God's rest has also rested from his works, as God did from His. Let us therefore strive to enter that rest, so that no one may fall by the same sort of disobedience.

ABUNDANT LIFE

Jesus said, "I am come that they might have life, and that they might have it more abundantly" (John 10:10 KJV). Note that He said He came not that you might have *church*, not that you might have *work*, or a *job*, or a *career*, but so that you may have life! Wow! So many people accomplish but never *live!* And a lot of people are uncomfortable because they don't know what living really means! What does living mean to you? Are you just looking for the next church service? Are you just looking for the next business deal, or the next vacation from a boring daily schedule? We have to work. We have to eat. We have to take care of our families. But is that all there is to life? All of us are looking for the next something. But Jesus came that we may have life. What a profound thought that is.

He came that you may have life—not merely the way you've been having it, but He wants you to know that there's a more excellent way for life to take place for you. He came that you might have it more abundantly, more fully, with nothing missing, nothing broken—all things intact. Abundance really means more than enough: that's the kind of life God always wanted us to have. He wants you to have more joy than you can handle, more peace than you could ever handle, more prosperity and more security than you've ever had, and a great sense of inner peace and an inner being that you've never had before. Jesus said, "I came that you might have all of that." More abundant life means life to the superlative. The *Message* translation refers to abundance as "to the full, until it overflows." I'm calling that life in the superlative.

The word *have* presupposes that Jesus came that I might lay claim on it, that I might possess it, and that I might obtain it, which suggests that there is a strategy for making it happen. There's a formula to follow. It does not just happen, because everybody doesn't have it. To have it, to obtain it, to possess it suggests that evidently, God has to give us a strategy to do so.

How do I possess it? How do I lay claim to it, put my hands on it? Well, first of all, Jesus said, "I came that you might have it." You know, it's already done! He finished that work; He's not going to do it again. It's already there! His words imply that you've got to have the right strategies that help you to understand how to live life in the superlative. They presuppose that I'm going to have to press toward what I've got to have and that I'm going to have to push toward what I've got to have.

Now, most books will tell you that you've got to work harder and you've got to do this and you've got to do that. But if Jesus already said I've got it, if He already came that I may have it, then that work is already done. So why am I working harder? Obviously, there's something *smarter* that I need to do. I've already been working hard. Working hard brought with it all of these other issues: health issues, family issues, and emotional issues. Some people lose the family because of all the overtime and extra work. Some folks lose their minds! I mean, honestly, some really smart people I know have lost it because of the stress of working too hard. They've lost their sense of direction. Many of them have lost their drive, and some have lost their determination.

Clearly, we need strategies for working *smarter* that will lead us to the abundant life already prepared for us.

OUR SEARCH FOR PURPOSE

In my estimation, abundant life for you and me is ultimately the product of fulfilled purpose. We're all on a very important journey, the essential quest of every life: finding a sense of purpose for the unique life each of us lives. But many people never find the answer. Many people never discover themselves. I've seen many people in Detroit follow what used to be a very common path: they started work in the auto plants, made a good salary, and decided never to go back to school. They told themselves, *I got out of high school, I got a job at the plant, and I've been here ever since. I'll never finish my education. I've got a good job now; I'll just keep rolling with this.* Today we would call those folks fortunate, because the great pay and great benefits they received without prior training are largely a thing of the past. Yet some of them never found their true purpose. They ran it all the way out, for thirty years or more.

Very often, the biggest interruption to the discovery of one's purpose is life itself! So many of us might say, "I was in pursuit of my destiny until I got married. We had kids. I had to get a better job." And sometimes we confuse our professional lives, our vocations, or our work lives with our purposes. Many times they don't have anything to do with each other. You don't even know what you're made of until you've had to navigate through a crisis. Until you've had some serious bumps in the road, you don't even know what you're capable of. You don't know what your character will accommodate until you are proven.

Every profession has a proving ground. In medicine, in manufacturing, in social services, in whatever kind of work you're doing, you have to prove that you can do the job *on the job*. If you're totally ineffective, then you lose credibility. If you open up a lemonade stand and the lemonade isn't sweet, you're going to be out of business.

People of faith and even those without it figure out the right direction for their lives after honest soul-searching. They ask for God's wisdom and guidance, or they simply search their own minds and hearts for the answer to eternal questions such as, *Why was I born? Why am I here? What am I here to do?* Finding a sense of purpose is important. But along that way we overwork ourselves trying to find it. We overcompensate, we overschedule, we become people-pleasers, we become back-scratchers.

We become people who fit in the machinations of other folks' needs. We make other people rich.

I can think of some examples from my own life when I supported others and I got crumbs or nothing in return. In addition, there were potentially lucrative opportunities that I have passed by because they did not fit my purpose. For instance, a group of good friends and associates asked me to become a founding partner of one of the large, successful casinos in downtown Detroit. I told them that I couldn't do it because it was against my ethical standards. I don't believe in games of chance. I'm not a gambler, and I don't believe in taking advantage of people because of their weaknesses. I'm sorry to say that I fell out with a particular friend who was already a partner in the venture. But it just wasn't the investment for me. I couldn't live with myself if I were invested in a business that encourages poor people to waste or risk their hard-earned money. One thing that is missing in the world today is ethics. So I am good with my decision.

THE CURVEBALL THAT PUT ME ON A STRAIGHT PATH

Life is often a very enigmatic thing. Just when you think you know your purpose and have a clear sense of it within your grasp, life becomes elusive. It throws you a curve and becomes enigmatic and hard to explain. In my case, I brought a lot of health challenges upon myself. My faith brought me through my crisis, then helped me to understand that I could overcome even the self-sabotage that I had orchestrated.

So I've learned lessons. When that curtain fell, a brand-new learning process for me began. A brand-new reassessment of life began. I experienced a paradigmatic shift in how I viewed who I am and what I do.

So I've made the needed modifications to my life and my lifestyle. I get my rest. I take time off that I never took off before. I take vacations that I never took before. I've shortened my workday. Whereas I used to run here and there, trying to do so many things by myself, I've learned how to delegate my professional responsibilities in a much better way. I've been cured of the "if I don't, it won't" syndrome.

I've learned how to focus on a few things and do them well, extremely well. And I no longer try to be all things to all people. Not long ago, I posted the following statement on Facebook: "I used to care *way* too much about people's opinions of me—until I tried to pay a bill with their thoughts."

What else is different with me now? My eating habits have changed. My sleeping habits have changed. My thought processes have changed. I'm not saying that I have conquered all of my professional and personal challenges. "I count not myself to have apprehended," as the apostle Paul writes in Philippians 3:13. This is a life's work: becoming who you're supposed to be in the way you're supposed to be.

I don't maintain that we can find that out at age twenty-five. Some twenty-five-year-olds might argue with me, but I have my doubts that those arguments would be persuasive. I think that life is a process of finding out *what* your destiny is, what your real purpose is.

My hope is that you will take inventory of the things that you do to yourself deleteriously, the things that harm you in the long run. Be willing to drop the things that don't matter nearly as much as you think they do or once thought they did. I urge you to do a reassessment of what the big priorities of life are, and then live a life that is a whole lot less dependent on what people think of you and a whole lot more dependent on what God has intended for you. Once you've identified a path that gives you peace and satisfaction in your mind and heart, accept it as His purpose and plan—and embrace His provisions to make those things happen.

In the end, to rely upon yourself is really an insult to God. To be at a point where you're depending only on you, and where you believe that nothing can work unless you work it, unless you do it—that's really an abrogation of faith. It's an insult to a God who created us with purpose yet to be fulfilled. While we're spinning our wheels, spinning plates with ancillary things, while we're majoring in minors, there is something higher in all of us, something great that is yet to be revealed.

THE EPILOGUE

<u>"Epilogue"</u> – is a piece of writing at the end of a work of literature, usually used to bring closure to the work. It is presented from the perspective of within the story – Wikipedia.

As pastor for over 41 years, I have often stood at the bedside of the terminally ill who are approaching life transition. It is a delicate, yet critical part of my work. The interface of saddened loved ones, the myriad of medical accoutrements, the guarded observations and tone of doctors and staff, and the deteriorating condition of the patient, all combine for a precariously uncertain setting. As I gently and compassionately seek to attend to the spiritual needs of the patients and loved ones, I normally, if possible engage in conversation with the patient. Many times as I have had these life-ending dialogues with those in transition, the patients share things with me unvarnished. At this point, there is nothing to prove and no one to impress. Never have I heard one of them say, "my greatest regret is that I didn't spend more time at work," or "I wish I had spent more of my time being busy."

What I've heard most often is that there was not enough time to focus on the things that really mattered. Family. Relationships. Leisure. Travel. Hobbies. Grandchildren. The key point to be remembered is that we must live a life of as few regrets as possible, while never losing our zest for it. The joy of life is probably more about the continuum of the journey, than it is about reaching a destination. So when you look back on your life, you will have accumulated joys and positive experiences, not defeat or unfulfillment.

The propriety of self-care is not only practical, it is inherently spiritual. Our bodies are a stewardship requiring accountable management. They are a divine investment by a benevolent Creator, for which there is an expectation of return. In the financial world, a trust is a fiduciary relationship in which one party holds the title deed signifying ownership of assets or property, for the use and benefit of another. In a spiritual context, God, The Creator, is The Owner and our bodies are a precious gift to us – the beneficiaries. We, the beneficiaries, are entrusted with the gift of our bodies. It is that gift that comes with an expectation of accountability.

Along my challenging health journey, I had to excogitate a fresh new algorithm, both in thought and practice. Much can be said about the power of thought and its ability to alter the trajectory of outcomes. Our minds are so powerful. The human brain is the most powerful computer ever created. With its 100 million neurons and quadrillion synapses wiring all these cells together, the brain is extraordinarily complex. Neuroscientists believe that the processing power of the human brain has the capacity to perform at a virtually infinite rate.

The concept of power, especially in the Bible, is clear and delineated in multiple ways. For example, that we receive all essentials according to *II Peter 1:3*, which says, *"….His divine power has given us everything we need for life……"* (New Revised Standard Version). So then, power coupled with thought ought to be an unstoppable combination. Right? "For as he thinks in his heart, so is he" (Proverbs 23:7a New King James Version). My question to myself was if, in fact, I had the benefit of all this power, why did I not make better choices? It was as if I saw a sign that said, "BRIDGE OUT AHEAD," and instead of pumping my brakes, I accelerated even more!

The power of choice impacts this dilemma: Our lives are the results of two things – making choices and taking chances. My experience was not only organic, it was pedagogical. Often, necessary decisions are deferred by simple indecision. The mistaken notion is that maybe if I ignore that warning signs, nothing will manifest. It will all disappear. But indecision is in reality, a decision. You can't blame anyone or anything for making unwise decisions. You can't play the victimization role and lay the blame for poor stewardship of the body on someone else.

So what is this new algorithm? What is this new cadence? New rhythm? It is a more thoughtfully harmonious and integrated life regimen. I do not engage in the proverbial war of work-life balance which presupposes the two entities, work and life, contending for dominance. Jeff Bezos, the CEO of Amazon is quite eloquent on this subject. He says, that work-life balance is a "debilitating phrase." He believes that work and life are not strict trade-offs. Instead, Bezos thinks of his personal and professional pursuits as a "circle," rather than a "balancing act."

I have learned to differentiate more distinctly what really matters. A new prioritization producing a fresh set of essentials has emerged. I have discovered that "busy" is overrated. The real issue often is not vision and creativity, it's disciplined execution. How much precision can you have if your plate is already full? So I've made necessary adjustments to better manage health, family, stress, business and professional responsibility.

The old adage is prophetic. "Everything else will survive, if you do." I have harnessed the power of spirituality and the power of the mind, to make better choices and decisions. One source of inspiration that lifted me is the book, "Essentialism," by New York Times and Wall Street Journal bestselling author, Greg McKeown. McKeown eloquently presents the case for systematic discipline on the discernment of what is absolutely essential in one's life. He then proposes we acquire the temerity to eliminate everything that is not. McKeown suggests that we move from a "non-essential list" mindset (not being able to discern and prioritize what is truly important) to an "essentialist" mindset. In doing so, we not only make our lives manageable, but we actually increase productivity and get more things done.

So I've checked many of the usual boxes. New attention goes to diet and exercise. I've reduced sodium, intake dramatically. I've cut out sugar-induced and high fructose beverages. I've increased fruit and vegetable intake. I've heightened my romance with my all-time favorite – WATER. I've stabilized my vitals. I've discovered the value of rest, relaxation, repositioning and rejuvenation in mind, body and spirit.

I did it to myself. But, thank God, I lived to tell my story. The grace of God miraculously kept me when I couldn't keep myself. Confucius, the Chinese philosopher, was once quoted as saying, "We get two lives, and the second one begins when we realize we only have one" Start again today. Reinforce thought with execution. C.S. Lewis, the heralded theologian once said, "You can't go back and change the beginning, but you can start where you are and change the ending." The game is never won in the first half. You actually win the game in the last quarter or the final inning.

I walked through the valley of the shadow of death. My journey, for me, inculcated a new revelation of Psalm 23:4 (Amplified Bible). "Even though I walk through the sunless valley of the shadow of death, I fear no evil, for you are with me. Your rod (to protect) and Your staff (to guide) they comfort and console me." I walked through that valley of the shadow of death, only to discover several things. First, I walked <u>THROUGH</u> it. It was not my permanent place. It was a passage designed to develop me and not destroy me. It was an excursion to the low extremity of existence, and yet through all of it I had no reason to fear because God was with me. Body unwell. Health compromised. Yet, I still walked through. Secondly, I walked through the valley of the shadows of death. A frightening reality. Literally, I experienced death, no heartbeat, no pulse, but again it was merely the shadow. God gave me a special gift, and I lived to tell the story.

My life was abruptly interrupted, so I could walk in the recesses of the valley, experience the darkness and deal with the shadows.

But most of all, the most salient reality in my "valley experience" is the indisputable, unassailable, incontestable presence and providence of God. I traversed in the uncertainty of the valley and survived the odyssey of death's shadows without fear. This kind of resolve is only possible with the confident commitment and assurance that God is with me. My faith is forever increased. My confidence is overwhelming. My determination is unparalleled.

I was not only secured and protected by God, but God gave me a support system to reinforce the reality of that presence. My wife, Sheila, is a treasured force of faith and comfort in the valley. Exuding a love for me that has stood the test of time. The magnitude of her heart is unsurpassed. My children prayed for me in emergency rooms and brought me cheer in lonely times. My congregation has loved me for over 41 years and blessed me greatly. The older I get, the more relationships mean to me. I value loyalty in relationships across racial, socioeconomic, business and cultural lines. Relationships are wind beneath my wings.

And though "I did it to myself," my experience in the valley did something significant for others as well. The hand of God and Hands-on

Cardio Pulmonary Resuscitation (CPR) gave me the opportunity to live and tell my story. Two of the senior registered nurses of my congregation, Erica Terry and Felicia Foster-Gibson, and our Emergency Medical Response Team, used their professional expertise to help bring me back.

The American Heart Association had been pushing legislation in the state of Michigan to require all students in our state to be taught CPR by the time they graduate. This was an ambitious piece of legislation to be pushed in a politically polarized environment in Lansing, our state's capitol. Thirty-four states have already adopted this as a law, but in Michigan, this needed initiative aimed at saving potentially thousands of lives, remained stalled for 18 months. State Senator Tonya Shuitmaker (R-Lawton) introduced Senate Bill 647 to codify this into law. Based on my valley experience, I was asked to lend my voice and influence toward this legislation. In our state, there is not just political polarization between Democrats and Republicans, but there is a regional polarization as well. This bill needed influence and support from southeast Michigan and the Detroit area where I reside. I joined forces with this movement and the legislation finally passed. I was present in our State Capitol for the signing of this bill by the Governor of the State of Michigan. Now, every student who finishes high school in the state of Michigan must complete a training in Hands-on Cardiopulmonary Resuscitation as a requirement for graduation. This has likelihood of saving thousands of lives, just like mine, in the years to come.

(Pics from articles)

Knowing that my personal journey will be redemptive and enlightening in the lives of so many others is a confirmation of purpose. In spite of the things I've done well and the things I've not done so well, a higher purpose has been manifested. So embrace life. Share Joy. Know your body. Stay alert. Be accountable. Blend work with life. Integrate life with work. Eliminate the non-essentials. Love life. Love God.

The Rev. Edgar Vann's Live-Saving Efforts Bear Fruit In Michigan

Carol Cain Detroit Free Press Business Columnist Updated 9:15 p.m. EST Dec. 31, 2016

Sometimes it takes a village, or in this case a bishop, an organization dedicated to the cause and a few elected officials working together to get legislation approved that will have Hands-Only CPR finally taught in Michigan schools.

Proponents teamed up in support of the life-saving legislation, which was signed by Lt. Gov. Brian Calley on Wednesday.

With Calley's signature, Michigan becomes the 36th state in which Hands-Only CPR will be taught to every student before they graduate from high school. The law takes effect in September when the new school year starts. The type of CPR being taught does not require certification or mouth-to-mouth resuscitation.

I wrote of the legislation a few months ago and <u>focused on the Rev. Edgar Vann</u> who had his own experience with cardiopulmonary resuscitation.

RELATED STORIES:

<u>Bishop Edgar Vann's close call leads to a push for student CPR training</u>
<u>Bill would require students to learn CPR</u>

He suffered a major heart attack after delivering a sermon to his congregation at Second Ebenezer Church in Detroit last New Year's Eve.

Coincidentally, Vann had decided to have church members trained in CPR for every church event some years ago, and it saved his life.

Vann became a champion for the legislation that the American Heart Association of Michigan has been advocating for the past 18 months. Also joining in the mission were legislators including state Sen. Tonya Schuitmaker, R-Lawton.

"Having more young people learn CPR will help to save many more lives in the years to come," said Vann.

Indeed, nearly 357,000 people suffer cardiac arrest outside of a hospital each year. And only 8% survive. But CPR can sometimes help.

"CPR can nearly triple survival rates for cardiac arrest by providing assistance until the EMTs arrive," said Sarah Poole, government relations director of the American Heart Association.

With the new legislation , there will be 100,000 students in Michigan learning Hands-Only CPR each year.

"Passage of this legislation was the result of hundreds of individuals who cared enough to contact their lawmakers, shared information with their family and friends, shared their stories of loss and/or survival after cardiac arrest," said Schuitmaker.

She will be on hand Tuesday with others involved in getting the legislation passed during a ceremonial signing of the legislation in Lansing.

Carol Cain can be reached at 313-222-6732 or clcain@cbs.com. She is senior producer/host of "Michigan Matters," which airs at 11:30 a.m. Sundays on CBS 62. See L. Brooks Patterson, Denise Ilitch and Mark Hackel on today's show.

Bishop Edgar Vann's close call leads to a push for student CPR training

Carol Cain Detroit Free Press Business Columnist 10:36 p.m. EDT Sep. 3, 2016

Bishop Edgar Vann was stepping down from the pulpit of Second Ebenezer Church in Detroit after preaching to his congregation this past New Year's Eve when he was confronted with death.

"It was as if a dark curtain was falling and I could feel myself losing consciousness and falling out," the 60-year-old said. "I turned to my wife and grabbed her and that's the last thing I remember."

Had it not been for someone in his congregation who administered cardiopulmonary resuscitation (CPR) immediately, he wouldn't be alive today.

"My heart stopped and there was no pulse," Vann said.

Heart disease is the No. 1 killer of Americans.

RELATED:BILL WOULD REQUIRE STUDENTS TO LEARN CPR

Years earlier, in what now seems very forward thinking, Vann decided to have people at his church trained in emergency measures like CPR. The church had been growing to more than 6,000 members and had moved to larger quarters. It just seemed important.

As a result of his experience, Vann has become a champion of CPR, more specifically a kind called Hands-Only CPR, and is pushing legislation, supported by others and the American Heart Association, that would require students in Michigan to be taught CPR by the time they graduate from high school.

Hands-Only CPR includes pressing on the chest and has shown to be as effective as conventional CPR when performed by a lay person. Conventional CPR includes breathing into a victim's mouth.

Thirty-four states have adopted such laws.

The Michigan legislation, called Senate Bill 647, was introduced by Sen. Tonya Schuitmaker, R-Lawton, and was passed with bipartisan support in May. It awaits a vote in the House when legislators return from summer break.

A second bill, House bill 5610, introduced by Rep. Tom Hooker, R-Byron Center, reads similarly and passed out of the House Education Committee. But the full House has not voted on it yet.

"Since the Senate bill is advancing more quickly, we are focusing on that bill," said Sarah Poole, government relations director of Michigan, American Heart Association.

"We are asking House members to make passing the legislation a priority in September so it can advance on to the governor for his signature," she added.

While the legislation seems like a good idea, it has its critics. Some lawmakers say cash- and time-strapped schools should be focusing on the ABC's of education — not teaching CPR.

In addition, there is the concern about resources associated with the program — time and money, which doesn't add up for schools.

Rep. Ed McBroom, R-Vulcan, a former school teacher from the Upper Peninsula, voted against the House bill when it was in committee last spring.

"It's a great idea," McBroom said, "but we are trying to mandate too much. It can get overwhelming. It's difficult legislation to say 'no' to in this political season. But sometimes as a legislator, you have to. Where does it stop?"

McBroom, who is term-limited, expects the measure will eventually be passed, as "some members will vote 'yes' saying it's not worth the political battle."

The American Heart Association counters that the training could cost as little as 60 cents per student. They say police and fire departments as well as hospitals could be asked to volunteer to reduce training costs.

But some just don't see the point.

"We have no business dictating classes that don't involve the business of education," said Rep. Ken Yonker, R-Caledonia, who voted no on the bill when it was in committee. "There are already health classes where teachers or volunteers are teaching CPR."

Yonker added, "I've had CPR training four or five times and I would not feel comfortable administering it."

"This legislation isn't going anywhere," he predicted.

A DIFFERENT WAY TO SAVE A LIFE

Hands-Only CPR training takes about 30 minutes and could be incorporated into existing health curriculum, supporters say.

If approved, the legislation and ensuing training would create 100,000 young people each year trained to potentially help those in distress.

Conventional CPR includes mouth-to-mouth resuscitation and exerting pressure on the chest.

Those squeamish about performing mouth-to-mouth may be more likely to consider Hands-Only.

"Each year, about 357,000 Americans suffer sudden cardiac arrest outside of a hospital, and only about 8% of these victims survive," said Catherine Smith, executive director of the southeast Michigan American Heart Association.

It's the first few minutes after an attack where CPR is crucial.

"We can nearly triple the odds of survival by providing effective CPR assistance until first-responders arrive," she added.

Schuitmaker, who introduced the Senate bill, said the 2011 death of a Fennville High School student athlete from sudden cardiac arrest while playing basketball served as a catalyst for her to get involved.

Her bill requires schools to add 30 minutes of Hands-Only training to their curricula for students somewhere between seventh and 12th grades.

In addition, students would be given information about using the automated defibrillators that are located in many schools.

"It's important that people be instructed to know how to use them so they're not scared when an emergency happens and they know what to do," Schuitmaker said.

Meanwhile, Vann is living healthier today as he continues his work with his church and other things in the community.

Besides his support of the Hands-on CPR legislation, he also is aiming to help others through a new book he is writing about his experience.

He wants to sound the alarm for other hard charging Type-A people who don't pay enough attention to their health, he said. He learned that lesson the hard way.

"A part of my healing process is a book that I am presently writing," he said. "I'm going to use my story in the book to help lift what happened to me as an example of me, by the grace of God, being given another chance to help other people understand the seriousness of heart disease."

Contact Carol Cain: 313-222-6732 or clcain@cbs.com. She is senior producer/host of "Michigan Matters" airing 11:30 a.m. Sundays on CBS 62. See Sean Larkins, Bishop Edgar Vann, Dr. Sinhu Koshy and Sarah Poole on today's show.

Printed in the United States
By Bookmasters